Cambridge Elements ☰

Elements in Politics and Society in East Asia
edited by
Erin Aeran Chung
The Johns Hopkins University
Mary Alice Haddad
Wesleyan University
Benjamin L. Read
University of California, Santa Cruz

POLITICAL SELECTION IN CHINA

Rethinking Foundations and Findings

Melanie Manion
Duke University

T0311517

Shaftesbury Road, Cambridge CB2 8EA, United Kingdom

One Liberty Plaza, 20th Floor, New York, NY 10006, USA

477 Williamstown Road, Port Melbourne, VIC 3207, Australia

314–321, 3rd Floor, Plot 3, Splendor Forum, Jasola District Centre, New Delhi – 110025, India

103 Penang Road, #05–06/07, Visioncrest Commercial, Singapore 238467

Cambridge University Press is part of Cambridge University Press & Assessment, a department of the University of Cambridge.

We share the University's mission to contribute to society through the pursuit of education, learning and research at the highest international levels of excellence.

www.cambridge.org
Information on this title: www.cambridge.org/9781009327114

DOI: 10.1017/9781009327145

First published 2023

A catalogue record for this publication is available from the British Library

ISBN 978-1-009-45419-3 Hardback
ISBN 978-1-009-32711-4 Paperback
ISSN 2632-735X (print)
ISSN 2632-7368 (online)

Political Selection in China

Rethinking Foundations and Findings

Elements in Politics and Society in East Asia

DOI: 10.1017/9781009327145
First published online: August 2023

Melanie Manion
Duke University
Author for correspondence: Melanie Manion, melanie.manion@duke.edu

Abstract: Political selection is about how individuals are selected to political office – and this substantially determines the quality of governance. The evidence favors democratic elections as the selection institution that produces high governance quality. Yet authoritarian China, where a communist party monopolizes the selection of all officials of importance, presents a sophisticated and, by some measures, successful contrast to liberal democratic versions of political selection. Understanding how and how much the preferences of the few at the political center in Beijing systematically shape the composition and actions of the tens of thousands of leaders who manage politics, society, and the economy across China is foundational to understanding China. This Element critically reviews the literature on political selection in China to better structure our knowledge on this important question. It clarifies sources of greatly disparate findings in statistical studies and identifies major descriptive challenges to these studies in rich qualitative and quantitative evidence.

Keywords: political selection, China, meritocracy, patronage, performance evaluation

ISBNs: 9781009454193 (HB), 9781009327114 (PB), 9781009327145 (OC)
ISSNs: 2632-7368 (online), 2632-735X (print)

Contents

1 Introduction

Institutions of political selection define whose preferences matter for the important question of who wields political power – and this substantially determines the characteristics of public officials and the quality of governance. Most fundamentally, these institutions distinguish liberal democracies from authoritarian states. Over a broad sweep of history, the evidence favors the principle of democratic elections as the selection institution that produces high governance quality (see Besley and Reynal-Querol 2011). Even so, in the contemporary world, authoritarian China presents a sophisticated and, by some measures, successful contrast to any liberal democratic version of political selection. Understanding how and how much the preferences of the few at the political center in Beijing systematically shape the composition and actions of the tens of thousands of leaders who manage Chinese politics, society, and the economy across the country is foundational to understanding China.

Paradoxically, however, at the same time as scholarship on political selection in China has greatly flourished in recent years, the research contours of this important question have shrunk. The study of political selection in China has become practically synonymous with the statistical analysis of promotion of subnational (mostly provincial) leaders, who are modeled as participants in starkly institutionalized yardstick competition with jurisdictional peers for career advancement as top economic performers. Studies focus on estimating how well local gross domestic product (GDP) growth predicts promotion and thereby explains the Chinese "economic miracle" of the 1980s and after. The dominant challenge to this economic tournament model analyzes career advancement – and indeed Chinese politics more generally – as distinctly *not* institutionalized. Instead, it estimates how well personal connections in the political elite determine who gets ahead. In this Element, I rethink foundations and findings in this literature on political selection in China, guided by lessons from fieldwork and views from the inside, some from my own work and many more from work by other scholars. My aim is to critically review and better structure our knowledge on this question.

Specifically, I clarify the sources of greatly disparate findings in foundational and later statistical studies and identify major descriptive challenges to these studies in rich qualitative and quantitative evidence. The challenges provide building blocks for a different way of thinking about how and why Chinese officials get ahead or merely get along in their careers. I propose a "good-fit" analytical perspective that takes the challenges into consideration. The perspective considers political selection as highly institutionalized – but also finds a place for the significant heterogeneity of standards by which official performance is evaluated in China. It identifies on-the-ground institutional flexibility by powerful communist party organization departments as integral to the design and practice of political selection in China.

1.1 The Notion of Political Selection

Political selection is about how individuals are selected to political office rather than how they are motivated or constrained once in office. For example, in liberal democracies, consistent with an underlying normative ideal of popular representation, multiparty elections are the institution by which voters select policymakers and legislators, even though political parties select the candidates for competition in most democracies (Hazan and Rahat 2010). Whatever its actual workings, the liberal democratic ideal in political selection is a design intended to empower each voter to choose his or her preferred politicians through competitive elections (Key 1966; Mayhew 1974; Fiorina 1981; Buchanan 1989; Manin 1997). This story is different from the notion of elections as an accountability design, which is about preventing politicians from engaging in self-dealing once elected. Besley (2005) observes that modern political economy has neglected the problem of political selection, instead focusing more on incentives that keep politicians accountable in office.

For bureaucrats in liberal democracies, the selection principle is different: they are appointed and their tenure in office is secured through institutions intended to realize an underlying normative ideal of meritocracy, not representation. As with elections, the agency problem looms large in the literature on bureaucratic discretion (e.g., Brehm and Gates 1997; Gailmard 2002; Whitford 2002; Balla and Gormley 2017) – but again, that is a story about control of how bureaucrats exercise delegated authority in office, not their selection to office.

Political selection in China presents a stark contrast to the allocation of selection power to voters in the liberal democratic ideal of representation. More than fifty years ago, Barnett (1967) identified communist party control over all careers of any importance from top to bottom as the "linchpin" of party rule in China; despite vast change in China since then, the description remains basically accurate. As elaborated in Section 1.3, the hierarchically organized ruling communist party monopolizes the appointments, promotions, transfers, and dismissals of bureaucrats and formally elected politicians.[1] The party center in Beijing directly manages a few thousand individuals in Beijing and the

---

[1] It extends to a wide range of individuals not strictly relevant to the study of political selection – for example, managers of state-owned enterprises, presidents of public universities, and administrators of state hospitals and public schools. This breadth reflects the formal reach of the Chinese state, even today.

provinces; it delegates the management of others to governing communist party committees below it.

In this sense, all Chinese leaders are like the bureaucrats in liberal democracies. This selection arrangement does not itself make Chinese officialdom a contemporary example of the meritocratic ideal; that requires, at least notionally, transparent communication and impartial application of standards of competence in personnel decisions. It does, however, allow for the possibility of it in authoritarian China – an idea that is politically provocative, even as a theoretical proposition.

The degree to which actual political selection measures up to the normative ideal is an empirical question. Bell (2015) develops the idea of political selection in contemporary China as meritocracy.[2] He points to a history of more than 1,300 years of competitive examinations for public officials in imperial China as a cultural basis for an idea that "political theorizing should be concerned with the question of how to select political leaders with superior abilities and virtues" (Bell 2015, 66). Imperial China's answer to the problem of selecting the competent and virtuous was the content of examinations: long study of the Confucian classics, necessary for examination success, inculcated the desired qualities for officials.[3] Political selection organized around the ideal of meritocracy, rather than representation, has important implications for the relationship between regime performance and regime legitimacy. For example, in a liberal democracy, incompetent or corrupt politicians can be replaced at the polls; by implication, voters are to blame for the political winners the elections produce. In authoritarian China, by contrast, widespread corruption and other serious performance failures pose an existential threat to the ruling communist party, which monopolizes political selection. If political selection in authoritarian China is done well enough, however, it may effectively compensate for the inadequacy of other institutions to monitor official behaviors and punish abuses of official power (Manion 2018).

---

[2] Bell goes further than the mere idea. He argues that public service examinations, which recruit officials to lower levels of government in China, reflect political meritocracy in practice, although he seems to recognize that such examinations are not used to select the political generalists who manage the party and government (Bell 2015, 78, 103). He also points out that the university entrance examination system, success in which is now required for political appointments, is perhaps "the least corrupt political institution in China" (Bell 2015, 87). These are empirical, not theoretical, arguments.

[3] There is an excellent extensive English-language literature on China's imperial examination system. See, for example, Miyazaki (1976), Herbert (1988), Chaffee (1995), Elman (2000), De Weerdt (2007), and Pines (2012). The debate on examination content was resolved differently over dynasties and across ranks, but Confucian classics figured large for most examinations in Chinese imperial history.

The notion that contemporary Chinese political selection is in principle meritocratic is provocative not only for its implied normative superiority to liberal democratic institutions but also (more subtly) because it implies that Chinese elite politics is institutionalized. This claim runs counter to a large literature that views Chinese politics as organized around networks of personalized factions, held together with patronage connections devoid of any substantive policy content (e.g., Nathan 1973; Pye 1980; Dittmer 1995). These competing views undergird the two dominant paradigms in the literature on political selection in China.

The *performance paradigm* implies that the *formal* institutions of political selection described in Section 1.3 are working more or less as designed. The party center in Beijing articulates the qualities it values – notably, GDP growth – which give highly specific content to metrics that party committees at lower levels use in evaluating the performance of officials relative to their peers – and officials are promoted or not promoted accordingly. By contrast, the *patronage paradigm* implies that *informal* institutions – notably, personal connections – underlie decisions on political selection: the metrics and evaluation procedures are mere "parchment institutions" (Carey 2000) that do not structure expectations about appointments.

1.2 Party and Government Leaders in China

Chinese officials are distinguished by administrative rank and salary grade, but the most important distinction is between "leading" and "ordinary" officials (see Pieke 2009, 30–32). Leaders, not ordinary officials, are the focus of interest here. As is true of all authoritarian states, we have little knowledge about the process by which leaders at the very apex of power are selected.[4] For the most part, the literature on political selection in China does not apply to these individuals but to the selection of subnational leaders – about which we know quite a lot.

The Chinese state is organized in a hierarchy of parallel governing communist party committees and governments that exist at the political center in Beijing and below, in each of the mainland's 31 provinces, 332 cities, 2,853 counties, and 33,272 townships. Townships are nested in counties, counties in cities, and cities in provinces.[5] Two leaders – a communist party secretary and a head of

---

[4] On selection of the roughly two dozen leaders at the top, we do have some interesting autobiographical accounts, some of them written with the obvious bias of "losers" in power struggles. In English, Wu (2015, 222–293) draws on many insider sources in his excellent study. In English translation, see the compilation of documents edited by Nathan and Link (2001) and the "secret journal" of Zhao Ziyang (2009).

[5] A note on terminology: here and throughout this Element, provinces also include the five minority-dominant regions and four mega-cities; cities refer to prefectural-level [地级] cities and also include rural prefectures; counties also include county-level cities; townships also

government – wield chief executive political power at each level of the state hierarchy, with the party leaders more powerful and higher in rank than their government counterparts.[6] These party and government leaders constitute the Chinese political elite below the apex of power, broadly, but not too broadly, defined. The literature focuses nearly exclusively on them – as I do in this Element.[7]

Statistical studies rarely extend their analysis to leaders below the city because systematic biographical data are not easily available. Indeed, most statistical studies focus on provincial leaders. By contrast, because of limitations on gathering evidence through fieldwork, qualitative studies mostly focus on townships, the lowest rung of the state hierarchy. If we exclude township party and government leaders – who are usually not considered in the ranks of senior officials – the population of interest is roughly *6,400 individuals*, who manage China's provinces, cities, and counties at any given time.[8] Table 1 summarizes a few characteristics of these individuals.

Overall, at every level, Chinese party and government leaders are predominantly male, ethnically Han, highly educated, and fairly young. The education and age characteristics reflect valued qualities that the party center in Beijing set out as part of a broad set of reforms intended to be the "organizational guarantee" of a "high-quality cadre corps" (Manion 2008, 613) beginning in the early 1980s and codified more strictly in the 1990s. Mandated retirement and age guidelines associated with different administrative ranks have important effects on promotions, an issue discussed in Section 3.1. Han Chinese comprise 92 percent of the Chinese population. Ethnic minorities often hold government

---

include towns. Provincial capitals and a few other cities rank administratively above the prefecture level, but I follow the literature in including them here with prefectural-level cities. Villages in rural China and neighborhoods in urban China are crucial to grassroots governance, but they are not formally part of the state structure.

[6] For the most part, officials working in communist party structures are party members, but party membership extends far beyond party structures. Roughly, anyone of political importance is a party member. This is certainly the case for government leaders – but party members are found everywhere, across occupations and among college students. Communist party members in 2022 totaled nearly 97 million, with large numbers of young people and well-educated professionals (Rui 2022).

[7] A reasonable but more expansive conception of the political elite would include the whole roster of "core party leaders" (Zeng 2016, 75) at each level of the state hierarchy below the political center, namely standing committee members of governing party committees and all members of township governing party committees, which are too small to form standing committees. These party committees and their standing committees are headed by the party secretary, normally with the government head sitting concurrently as deputy party secretary. The same institutions of political selection apply to both this collection, perhaps about 260,000 in total, and the subset of chief executives. Ang (2016, 106) suggests an even more expansive occupation-based definition, which counts 500,000 public officials as the political elite. Most of these are not leaders, however. Liu (2018) includes the entire civil service as the political elite, about 7 million individuals. For an informative earlier discussion, see Brødsgaard (2004).

[8] Including township leaders, the total is roughly 73,000 individuals.

Table 1 Demographic characteristics of party and government leaders

	Province		City		County	
	Party	**Government**	**Party**	**Government**	**Party**	**Government**
Male	100%	88.9%	97%	93.4%	93%	90.7%
Han	92.6%	77.8%	92.2%	78.7%	86.3%	75.9%
Average age	65	60	56	53	52	49
College	96.3%	92.6%	94.9%	95.2%	57.7%	67.4%

Note: Figures for provincial and city leaders are for 2020; for county leaders, they are for 2018. College attendance includes special training programs organized for officials [干部专修科] by universities and communist party schools.

Source: Computed from data provided by Xiaoshu Gui, Duke University, and Pierre Landry, Chinese University of Hong Kong.

(but rarely party) leadership offices in jurisdictions where they constitute at least a plurality of the population. As to the predominance of males, women have never gained anything close to representation in the communist party, much less in leadership offices, despite regular policy pronouncements throughout the party's history supporting gender equality. At the apex of power, the Politburo Standing Committee has always been exclusively male. The somewhat larger Politburo has typically featured only one woman among its roughly two dozen members. The Politburo selected in 2022 features no women at all. The scarcity of women in political leadership across China plainly refutes any argument that China's political selection institutions are fundamentally meritocratic.[9]

1.3 Formal Institutions of Political Selection

Since the 1950s, as in the former Soviet Union, the communist party has managed its power over the careers of all individuals of any importance with a *nomenklatura* system (Manion 1985; Burns 1989, 1994, 2006; Huang 1995; Lam and Chan 1996; Brødsgaard 2004; Chan 2004; Landry 2008). This system assigns to governing party committees at each level of the state hierarchy the complete authority over appointments, promotions, transfers, and dismissals of officials one level down. The one-level-down principle was introduced in 1984, as part of the revival and reform of the *nomenklatura* system, which Mao abandoned in the Cultural Revolution in the 1960s and 1970s.[10] At the apex of power, the Politburo Standing Committee appoints approximately 100 state-level officials. Its Central Organization Department manages the appointments of provincial party and government leaders. Below the political center, provincial party committees appoint city party and government leaders, city party committees appoint county party and government leaders, and county party committees appoint township party and government leaders.[11]

At each level of the state hierarchy, the actual work of managing officials is conducted by communist party organization departments, whose heads are *ipso facto* members of the party standing committee. Organization departments

---

[9] Indeed, legal discrimination is also at work. Women have less time to advance their official careers before facing mandatory retirement: below the city level, women retire at age fifty-five, men at age sixty. See Section 3.1 and Table 5.

[10] The *nomenklatura* system adopted in the 1950s observed a two-levels-down principle, which was briefly revived in the early 1980s. Its greater span of central control facilitated the rehabilitation of officials purged across China in the Cultural Revolution. Once rehabilitation was basically completed, the party center substituted greater delegation and more regulation for direct control. The introduction of the one-level-down principle in 1984 reduced the number of officials on the party center's *nomenklatura* from about 13,000 to about 4,200 (Landry 2008, 45). For a brief history, see Manion (1985).

[11] More precisely, party committees appoint the "leading group" one level down. This includes deputy party secretaries and all other members of party standing committees.

collect, assess, and store information about officials. Organization department heads present cases to the full party committee, with recommendations for appointments, promotions, transfers, or dismissals. In this sense, the *nomenklatura* system makes communist party committees and their powerful organization departments the "selectorates" (and principals) of officials one level down. Given the formal requirement of Leninist party organizational discipline, which mandates compliance to superior organizations in the party hierarchy, this makes the party center in Beijing, with its general secretary and half-dozen Politburo Standing Committee members at the pinnacle, the supreme principal. The party center also controls official careers by setting standards for advancement, to reflect its policy priorities. The *nomenklatura* system, with its key organizing principle "the party manages cadres" [党管干部], is the scaffolding of formal institutions of political selection in China. In the post-Mao years, the party center has issued several sets of detailed regulations that establish how to vet and select leaders for career advancement.

As early as 1979, the Central Organization Department called for a formal system to evaluate performance, to be developed first as an experiment in several localities, with the goal of formalizing it within a few years. As Whiting (2004, 103) notes, this marked an important turn away from subjective assessments of political attitudes that had prevailed in previous decades toward "specific, measurable, and quantifiable indicators of performance." In 1995, the Central Organization Department followed up with specific standards to evaluate performance of township and county leaders, as an input into decisions on career advancement.[12] The arrangements explicitly encouraged competition across peers in the same jurisdiction. What became the "target responsibility system" [责任指标体系] was gradually implemented nationwide, with coverage extended to city leaders in 2005 (Whiting 2004; Gao 2015; Zuo 2015).

Under the target responsibility system, leaders sign contracts to fulfill highly specific performance targets. The targets are assigned weights, which vary across localities to reflect local priorities (see Edin 1998, 2003; Whiting 2000, 2004). Some targets contradict others. Moreover, as Bulman (2016, 155) observes, "the sheer number of targets in different fields makes promotions based on uniform comparable criteria nearly impossible." However, some targets are always and everywhere weighted more heavily. Indeed, targets for social order, population control, and economic growth are categorized as "imperative" [一票否决]: failure to achieve them disqualifies leaders for promotion. Performance rankings (but not scores) within the jurisdiction are public

---

[12] Chan and Gao (2008) translate and discuss the 1995 document, issued by the Central Organization Department on August 31. This is different from the Central Committee document issued on February 9, 1995, and discussed later in this section.

knowledge – which creates intense peer pressure. In addition to the implications of performance for career advancement, Gao (2015, 629) notes the "symbolic value" of a good ranking and Zuo (2015, 961) notes the "official disgrace" of a poor ranking. Performance does not affect basic salary but does determine bonuses, which can create big variation in compensation. For example, Whiting (2004) finds compensation for leaders of a suburban county in Shanghai ranges from 6,000 to 17,500 yuan in 1995, due to differences in measured performance.

Not surprisingly, the high-stakes performance evaluations at the core of the newly revived *nomenklatura* system also produce perverse outcomes. Most notable are various sorts of data manipulation and falsification (see Gao 2009, 2010, 2015; Kung and Chen 2011; Li 2015; Wallace 2016). For example, Wallace (2016) analyzes provincial gaming of economic targets and shows that the gap between reported GDP growth and objective measures of economic health, such as energy consumption, increases significantly around times of leadership turnover, as leaders produce records of accomplishment worthy of promotion.[13] Further down the state hierarchy, Gao (2015) argues that party committees lack the appropriate incentives to curb inflation of performance data by leaders over whom they have *nomenklatura* authority because their own performance results are similarly ranked.

The most important document for the political selection of leaders in China is *Regulations on the Selection and Appointment of Party and Government Leading Officials*, which the Central Committee issued first as a provisional document in 1995 and revised and reissued in 2002, 2014, and 2019.[14] The regulations apply to party and government leaders at and above the county level.

---

[13] Principals at the party center must suspect that local agents are "juking the stats." A US government cable exposed by WikiLeaks recounts a conversation with Li Keqiang, then executive vice premier. Li comments that GDP statistics are "man-made" and "therefore unreliable." He reportedly focuses instead on electricity consumption, volume of rail cargo, and loans disbursed to assess economic growth – and considers all other statistics, especially GDP statistics, "for reference only." WikiLeaks, Cable 07BEIJING1760, March 15, 2007. Cited in Wallace (2016).

[14] See Communist Party of China, Central Committee, February 9, 1995, *Provisional Regulations on the Selection and Appointment of Party and Government Leading Officials* [党政领导干部选拔任用暂行工作条例]: www.reformdata.org/1995/0209/4368.shtml; Communist Party of China, Central Committee, July 9, 2002, *Regulations on the Selection and Appointment of Party and Government Leading Officials* [党政领导干部选拔任用工作条例]: www.itp.cas.cn/djykxwh/llxx/dnfg/202011/t20201124_5777779.html; Communist Party of China, Central Committee, January 14, 2014, *Regulations on the Selection and Appointment of Party and Government Leading Officials* [党政领导干部选拔任用暂行工作条例]: http://renshi.people.com.cn/n/2014/0116/c139617-24132478.html; Communist Party of China, Central Committee, March 18, 2019, *Regulations on the Selection and Appointment of Party and Government Leading Officials* [党政领导干部选拔任用暂行工作条例]: http://cpc.people.com.cn/n1/2019/0318/c419242-30980036.html. As is common in the Chinese political system, the regulations instruct provincial party committees to develop comparable regulations governing the selection of township leaders.

All four versions of the regulations include highly specific stipulations about matters including qualifications for leadership, procedures for vetting by the organization department, rules of party committee decision-making on career moves, the importance of regular job rotation, and rules of avoidance to prevent officials from governing in localities where they grew up or where their relatives also work.

The processes of the evaluation and vetting [考核 and 考察] of leaders for promotion are more comprehensive than a mere assessment of target fulfillment [目标考核]. I elaborate on this in Section 4, but it is useful to note here that the regulations do not imply a simple rule of promoting the top economic growth performer. Achievements [绩] and competence [能] are key components of assessment, but GDP growth is by no means the only (or necessarily the crucial) achievement or indicator of competence.

1.4 Preview

The rest of this Element is organized as follows. Section 2 is the descriptive core of the work. It reviews the main literature on political selection in China. Its goal is to structure our understanding of the statistical studies that feature the career advancement of Chinese leaders as the dependent variable. The section, like the literature, is organized around the two dominant paradigms. The performance paradigm takes as its motivation the puzzle of China's rapid economic growth in the 1980s and 1990s. Its theory and findings attribute this growth to peer competition across subnational leaders, whose promotion depends on best performance, measured through the formal institutions described in Section 1.3. By contrast, the patronage paradigm views political selection as a matter of elite power politics. Leaders build and strengthen covert factional networks to gain and maintain power. Political selection is about advancing the careers of presumably loyal clients. The section considers and clarifies the sources of disparate findings in the studies: for example, not only do studies have different scope conditions but no two studies reflect the same collection of choices about model specification.

Sections 3 and 4 are responses to Section 2. Section 3 presents descriptive challenges from rich qualitative and quantitative evidence, much of it from fieldwork. Most straightforwardly, the evidence challenges some assumptions of dominant paradigms. More fundamentally, it suggests a different, more holistic way of thinking about political selection. Two descriptive challenges have to do with career patterns: age constraints and so-called lateral transfers. Not only are both observed as empirical regularities but they are also codified in the communist party regulations described in Section 1.3. Age constraints consist of mandated age-based retirement and graduated "age ceilings" that limit eligibility for promotion at each level of the administrative hierarchy. Age constraints imply that we cannot treat promotions within jurisdictions at the same level of the state hierarchy as yardstick competitions. Some proportion of officials can compete with peers to get ahead, but most face age constraints and can aspire merely to get along. We cannot treat this latter group as incentivized by the prospect of promotion. Lateral transfers present a different challenge: offices ranked as equal administratively are not necessarily equal in political importance. Some (plausibly substantial) numbers of lateral transfers are de facto promotions, although they are coded in the literature as "no change." This unresolved problem of measurement error poses a threat to causal inference in statistical studies. The more fundamental descriptive challenge is neither age constraints nor lateral transfers, however. It is the heterogeneity of standards by which official performance is measured. This appears in various forms: important parameters other than economic growth, different central policy priorities over time, and, most problematically, emphases on different parameters across localities at the same level of the state hierarchy. This last form of heterogeneity presents a major challenge to the statistical modeling of promotion.

Section 4 proposes an analytical perspective that takes seriously the descriptive challenges identified in Section 3 and differs from the dominant paradigms reviewed in Section 2. My "good-fit" perspective focuses on the expansive powers delegated to organization departments. Their assorted activities make up the core of the political selection process. The literature reviewed in Section 4 shows that political selection is comprehensive, complex, and nuanced. Organization departments exercise on-the-ground institutional flexibility, paying close attention to spatial, temporal, and individual specificity. Political selection is a nearly continuous process of cultivating a large pool of good-enough candidates and selecting from the pool the individuals who happen to be a good fit for the time and place, as offices open up. The perspective developed in Section 4 accepts the premise of the performance paradigm that political selection is highly institutionalized. It differs from that paradigm in a crucial way, however: it views the management of heterogeneity as integral to political selection.

Section 5 concludes by reflecting on our cumulated knowledge about political selection in China, from the statistical studies considered in Section 2 and the quantitative and qualitative studies considered in Sections 3 and 4. It also considers and contextualizes political selection under Xi Jinping. Xi ascended to supreme leadership of the communist party in 2012 and continues in that role still, flouting recent practice of two terms for the party general secretary.

2 Dominant Paradigms: What Have We Learned?

Two wholly different paradigms dominate statistical studies of political selection in China. They are motivated by distinct theoretical puzzles. In all of them, the dependent variable is career advancement, usually measured as promotion in administrative rank. As shown in Table 2, over the past quarter-century, we can interpret mean observed likelihood of promotion in any given year as ranging from 5 to 9 percent for party leaders and 13 to 18 percent for their government counterparts.[15]

The dominant perspective on political selection in China is the *performance paradigm*, prompted by China's extraordinary economic growth in the 1980s and 1990s: an average annual GDP growth rate exceeding 10 percent.[16] This "economic miracle" presents a theoretical puzzle for the political economy of authoritarianism. Authoritarian governments enforce property rights relatively weakly and provide fewer public goods than do democracies and, as a consequence, grow more slowly (Keefer and Knack 1997). China is no exception to the authoritarian pattern of weak property rights protection. The performance paradigm attributes China's rapid

Table 2 Promotions, 1996–2017

		Party	**Government**
Province	1996–2007	4.8	11.0
	2007–2017	5.6	15.8
City	1996–2007	13.6	11.0
	2007–2017	9.5	15.6
County	1996–2007	7.3	16.9
	2007–2017	9.2	14.5

Note: Figures in cells are percentages for party and government leaders in locality–year panels for the subnational levels and years indicated. For each cell, *all* career changes (i.e., promotions, transfers, dismissals, retirements, deaths) plus *no* change add up to 100 percent.

Source: Computed from data provided by Pierre Landry, Chinese University of Hong Kong.

---

[15] The percentages are based on the measure of promotion in Landry, Lü, and Duan (2018). Government leaders have more promotion possibilities because party leaders are senior to them at each level of the state hierarchy. A commonly observed career movement for government leaders is promotion to the position of party secretary in the same province, city, or county. For party leaders, a promotion to the next higher level in the state hierarchy is more competitive.

[16] This high GDP annual growth rate in fact continued through a third decade, after which it slowed. See Naughton (2007) and Barry Naughton, "Updated Data for the Chinese Economy" at www .barrynaughton.com/data/.

economic growth to structured peer competition across subnational leaders for career advancement based largely on performance in achieving local GDP growth. This story implies the formal institutions described in Section 1.3 work roughly as designed to realize the party center's strategic priority of economic growth set out in late 1978.[17]

The performance paradigm implicitly assumes China's leaders have long enough time horizons to motivate them to invest in the sorts of growth-enhancing institutions of political selection that undergird the paradigm. As Haber (2006) notes, this perspective seems to ignore fundamentals in the literature about politics under authoritarianism. The *patronage paradigm* takes up these fundamentals. The stakes of losing office under authoritarianism can be very high, but political conformity makes it difficult for leaders to discern loyal supporters because everyone professes support (Tullock 1987). Leaders gain and keep political power through patronage appointments, using their power over personnel to build networks of presumably loyal followers. Political selection outcomes are "pure power questions" (Pye 1980, 180).

This section reviews the perspectives and findings in statistical studies associated with each of the two paradigms. For expository clarity, I distinguish sharply between them – perhaps too sharply. More authentically, we might consider the paradigms as bundles of different intellectual priors and disciplinary tastes in estimating "effects of causes." That is, scholars working within the performance paradigm focus on estimating the specific effect of local GDP growth on promotions, but they would not likely reject the proposition that personal connections can also affect promotions. Similarly, scholars working within the patronage paradigm attempt to estimate the specific effect of personal connections on promotions, but they might not all reject outright the proposition that performance or, more broadly, formal institutions of political selection can also affect promotions. In this sense, most of the scholarship in both paradigms differs from a "causes of effect" approach to explaining promotions. I return to this issue in Section 2.5.

2.1 Tournament Competition for Economic Growth

The performance paradigm essentially attributes the remarkable growth achieved since the 1980s to a unique governance design of economically self-contained localities inherited from the late 1950s, what Xu (2011) labels "a relatively decentralized authoritarian system." More to the point, the story goes, in the reform

---

[17] That the story also reflects favorably on the party center in Beijing may account for the explosion in mainland China of scholarship on political selection, mostly adopting the performance paradigm. For example, looking at listings in the China National Knowledge Infrastructure (CNKI, in Chinese 知网) database, my research assistant Ying Chi finds 4,811 articles on political selection (选拔干部) in Chinese academic journals in the period 1990–2022.

era, with Beijing's new priority of economic growth and mandated routines of performance evaluation of state agents, the design pits subnational political chief executives against peers in tournament (yardstick) competition to impress their jurisdictional superiors with higher local GDP growth and thereby win promotion.

2.1.1 Theory

The tournament model in this story originates in classic studies by economists on the internal organization of the firm, particularly studies that identify and analyze the multidimensional (M-form) and unitary (U-form) corporate structures. The decentralized M-form firm is associated with greater efficiency and higher profits compared to the U-form firm, both in theory (Williamson 1975) and empirically, in the historical record of changing corporate structure in the United States in the first half of the twentieth century (Chandler 1962). The U-form firm features functionally specialized subordinate divisions, with top managers coordinating across interdependent divisions to produce some product. Its advantage is economies of scale. By contrast, the advantage of the M-form is its structuring of performance incentives: the M-form firm is constituted of like, self-contained, semi-autonomous divisions – which facilitates gauging the relative performance of division managers. Top managers can use benchmarks to set profit goals and monitor profitability across subordinate divisions, duly rewarding best performers. The M-form structures competition across division managers as a tournament of peers.

Qian and Xu (1993), in a pathbreaking essay, apply the language of institutional form to describe whole economies. They observe that China's political economy is structured like a "deep" M-form corporation, with its multiple layers of relative economic self-sufficiency, in territorial "pieces" [块], from the provinces down to the very lowest level of governance. This is completely different from the classic Soviet-style planned economy, where information and control flows hierarchically in "lines" [条], from functionally defined central ministries to subordinate enterprises grouped by industry, an arrangement the essay compares to a U-form corporation. China's cellular economy is a legacy of the Maoist era or earlier; importantly, post-Mao reformers adopted policies to deepen economic decentralization.[18] The essay's main argument is that the further decentralization of China's M-form economy facilitated a phenomenal expansion of the non-state sector – and this expansion largely accounts for the rapid growth of the 1980s and 1990s. The specific institutional logic the essay

---

[18] See Donnithorne (1972) for a discussion of China's cellular economy in the Maoist era. Xu (2011) goes further back, tracing the origins of China's regional decentralization to the imperial period.

describes is not itself new.[19] It works through several familiar economic mechanisms: decentralized fiscal arrangements that create incentives for townships and villages to set up enterprises, flexibility for local economic experimentation and diffusion of success, and a reduction in the scope of planning to allow for the emergence of markets. In this institutional logic, there is no need for the argument that the Chinese M-form economy creates incentives for growth by structuring competition across localities as a tournament of peers – and the essay does not elaborate such an argument.

The breakthrough for tournament competition as a mechanism that explains China's economic growth is Maskin, Qian, and Xu (2000). This study is important as a mathematical modeling exercise and as a first empirical application of the tournament model to political selection in China.[20] Maskin, Qian, and Xu (2000) begin with the Qian and Xu (1993) adaptation of corporate form to characterize whole economies, but they return to the classic theme that different organizational forms provide different information about managerial effort, on which incentives can be based. To motivate the analysis, they revisit the idea that M-form firms incentivize managers better than U-form firms do because their tournament structure allows top managers to better gauge and reward relative performance. They ask: Why do we intuitively not presume competition between industrial ministries in a U-form economy works the same way?

Analytically, the crux of the comparison between the two organizational forms has to do with noise in information about firm performance as a reflection of managerial effort. The noisier measured performance is as a function of effort, the more difficult it is to incentivize a manager to supply effort. For example, if exogenous shocks commonly affect measured performance, then performance-based incentives will not incentivize effort. Maskin, Qian, and Xu (2000) show mathematically that the M-form dominates the U-form from an incentive standpoint, so long as performance across two regions varies less than does performance across two industrial ministries. Whether this assumption holds is an empirical question, but they find some support for it in an examination of a sample of Chinese enterprises and regions.[21]

The important next step is to apply the tournament model to political selection. Maskin, Qian, and Xu (2000) note that relative performance evaluation appears to be widespread in China. They cite Whiting (1995) on the use of

---

[19] For example, see Oi (1992), which Qian and Xu (1993) cite.

[20] See Krugman (1993) on the importance of a model for a topic to achieve mainstream status.

[21] They estimate a model of relative industry-specific shocks and region-specific shocks for 520 state-owned enterprises in machinery, chemicals, and textiles distributed across 20 provinces in the period 1986–1991. The series has too few data points for a formal test, but they visually compare the estimated means of conditional variances for an M-form configuration with those for a U-form configuration. They find the former are generally smaller than the latter.

performance metrics in procedures to evaluate township officials. They then offer a simple test of the tournament model for provincial leaders. Specifically, they use provincial representation on the Central Committee, normalized by provincial population size, as a proxy for promotion chances for officials by province. They assemble data on provincial representation for 1977 and 1987 and data on provincial GDP growth rates for 1976 and 1986. They then rank provinces on each dimension for each year. They estimate a very basic regression model to analyze how change in relative ranking in economic performance is associated with change in relative ranking in Central Committee representation.[22] They find a significant positive correlation between the two, which, they argue, suggests an actually functioning tournament competition across provinces. That is, Chinese provincial leaders are incentivized by a governance design that pits them to compete against their peers to increase provincial GDP growth, which, in turn, produces China's economic miracle. This is very primitive but still remarkable as the first study to articulate and test the performance paradigm in China's political selection.[23]

In sum, Qian and Xu (1993) give us the valuable insight that China's cellular economy is structured much like a multilayered M-form corporation. Analytically, that this organizational form can work, as in firms, to incentivize local leaders in tournament competition with peers at each level of governance in China, as Maskin, Qian, and Xu (2000) propose, is plausible and appealing. It is also consistent with early studies of process in Chinese townships and with formal institutions of political selection introduced by the party center in 1995 and described in Section 1.3.

At the same time, whether the yardstick competition found in townships actually scales up to the province, the level at which most studies test it, is an empirical question. Beijing did not actually introduce a target responsibility system for leaders above the county level until after 2005. With no formalized process for economic tournament competition across provincial leaders, we must

---

[22] The model is underspecified. Even Li and Zhou (2005) observe that it suffers from omitted variable bias.

[23] Actually, Bo (1996) predates this empirical work with an analysis of determinants of promotion for provincial party secretaries and governors from the 1950s to the mid-1990s. He finds that leaders of bigger or wealthier provinces are more likely to be promoted but, on average, economic performance, measured in terms of both growth rates and revenue contributions to the political center, is negatively associated with upward mobility. Bo interprets this pattern as Beijing's preference to retain high-performing leaders in their positions. It is difficult, however, to defend any theoretically based priors about an "average" relationship between economic performance and career advancement over the decades before the 1990s for two main reasons. First, formal institutions of political selection were hardly articulated before the 1990s. Second, officially valued qualities for officials shifted dramatically from the 1950s to the 1980s, a period that includes the ideologically radical Cultural Revolution. Bo (2002) extends the analysis through 1998 and proposes a similar logic for findings.

presume these leaders worked "as if" evaluated and promoted on the basis of economic growth in their provinces – because the party center prioritized it.[24] This is not as fundamentally problematic for the Maskin, Qian, and Xu (2000) premises as the issue of unit size and, by implication, heterogeneity. Within counties, which are a much smaller land mass than are provinces, there may be significant unit homogeneity (e.g., a similar agricultural endowment). We can then assume shocks in any single county affect its townships roughly similarly, which implies that township economic outcomes roughly reflect the effort of township leaders. In this arrangement, tournament competition across townships can be incentivizing. However, across China's vast land mass, its thirty-one provinces exhibit huge interprovincial heterogeneity.[25] Shocks likely affect outcomes differently in different provinces. In this basic sense, the provinces resemble the different industrial ministries in Maskin, Qian, and Xu (2000), not townships or counties. Put another way, heterogeneity across geographic units cautions against scaling up.

2.1.2 Foundational Statistical Work

The theory underpinning the performance paradigm is appealingly simple and general. Also, the basic configuration of power in China's "relatively decentralized authoritarian system" (Xu 2011) seems unusually suited to it. Empirically, however, as shown in Section 2.3, its record as a predictive model is mixed. In this section, I focus on foundational statistical work.

The study by Li and Zhou (2005), now with more than 2,800 Google Scholar citations, offers the first systematic test that directly links economic performance and career advancement in China. It analyzes this relationship for a panel dataset of 254 provincial party and government leaders for the 1979–1995 period.[26] It finds a significant positive relationship between promotion and local GDP growth.

---

[24] Shirk (1993, 189) provides some evidence for this, on the basis of interviews with provincial leaders: "Under the post-1980 incentive structure, the political ambitions of local officials became closely identified with the economic accomplishments of their domains." Also, GDP growth targets in Five-Year Plans and annual plans were fairly high in the 1980s and especially after 1992. As Li, Liu, Weng, and Zhou (2019) show, provinces set their own growth targets 10–30 percent higher than central targets and set city growth targets 2–3 percent higher than provincial targets. As elaborated in Section 3.3.1, however, Beijing's growth priority was not constant. Hu Jintao, communist party general secretary in 2002–2012, introduced relatively greater attentiveness to social welfare, which Zuo (2015) shows was reflected in performance targets and promotion outcomes. Xi Jinping, Hu's successor, has prioritized a broad campaign against corruption.

[25] Obviously, due to their much larger size, we also expect much greater within-unit heterogeneity in provinces than in counties – but this is not analytically relevant here.

[26] Tibet and Hainan are excluded from the sample, the former because of its special political status, the latter because it attained provincial status only in 1988.

Li and Zhou (2005) frame the research as an incentives explanation for the growth-promoting behavior of subnational Chinese leaders, which contrasts with the rent-seeking observed in other transitional and developing countries.[27] Theoretically, the paper adopts the tournament competition model of Maskin, Qian, and Xu (2000) and points to anecdotal evidence in Whiting (2000) that shows Chinese leaders are indeed evaluated based on their economic performance. It specifies an ordered probit model to investigate the probability of promotion, termination, or no change for provincial party secretaries and governors.[28] This makes no scaling assumption of any kind. It only assumes promotion is more desirable than continuation at the same rank, which is more desirable than any form of termination.

For party secretaries, promotion is a vice premiership or premiership or membership on the State Council, Politburo, or Politburo Standing Committee. For governors, it is appointment as a provincial party secretary or equivalent-ranking position in a ministry or commission at the political center. The key independent variable of theoretical interest is provincial economic performance, measured in separate models as annual provincial GDP growth rate and average provincial GDP growth rate during the leader's tenure. Both analyses pool party and government leaders together.

In addition to standard individual-level covariates (education, age, tenure in office), the study controls for experience at the political center, measured as an indicator variable that equals 1 for leaders with a previous or concurrent appointment at the center and 0 otherwise. Such experience, it conjectures, can provide knowledge about the workings of appointment procedures and help cultivate informal connections with central leaders who can influence evaluations.[29] Models also take into account cyclical policy shocks and provincial characteristics, with lagged provincial per capita GDP and a set of provincial indicators.

Overall, Li and Zhou (2005, 1760–1761) present evidence to support the view that "the Chinese central government uses personnel control to motivate

---

[27] As the study observes, their perspective also contrasts with an explanation of Chinese economic growth based on the policy of fiscal decentralization and intergovernmental fiscal revenue-sharing contracts introduced in the 1980s. On this view, see Oi (1992) and Montinola, Qian, and Weingast (1995).

[28] Empirically, termination is largely age-based retirement for their sample, but a sensitivity test reassures us that findings of an economic performance effect are not mainly due to the retirement policy introduced in the early 1980s. The estimated effect of the policy in main regression models is significant and very large, however: reaching age 65 reduces the likelihood of promotion by 73 percent of the average probability of promotion. "No change" includes lateral transfer. On this issue, see Section 3.1.

[29] These logics and measure fall far short of the patronage model reviewed in Section 2.2. For one thing, every past and present connection at the political center is implicitly assigned the same weight. Experience at the political center is found to have a large effect.

local officials to promote local economic growth." Regressions using average growth rate and annual growth rate perform similarly. Both measures of economic performance have a significant and substantial positive effect, although promotions and terminations appear more sensitive to average growth rate.

In a follow-up study, Chen, Li, and Zhou (2005) use the same dependent variable but extend the analyses to 2002 and measure economic performance differently in three models as: moving average of provincial GDP per capita growth rates over the tenure of the provincial leaders, provincial GDP growth rate of the immediate predecessor, and GDP growth of neighboring provinces. They find that promotion of provincial leaders is associated not only with their own economic performance (as in Li and Zhou 2005) but also with the performance of immediate predecessors. They conclude that Beijing not only consciously motivates subnational leaders by linking their turnover to economic growth but also does so in a relatively sophisticated way to reduce noise. Specifically, Beijing "only puts weight on provincial benchmarks set by the immediate predecessor. The benchmark choice ... can be rationalized by the substantial disparity across provinces in China as well as concerns about the potential costs of non-cooperation generated by the tournaments among neighboring provinces" (Chen, Li, and Zhou 2005, 424–425). These are strong claims about design choices.

2.2 Patronage Connections for Political Survival

Where the performance paradigm is motivated by a puzzle in the political economy of development, the patronage paradigm considers political selection squarely as a question of elite politics. It responds to the theory and evidence associated with the performance paradigm by situating the question of political selection in a well-established older literature on factions in Chinese politics (e.g., Nathan 1973; Pye 1980, 1981; Dittmer 1995; Nathan and Tsai 1995; Tsou 1995) and mostly emphasizing the structural influences of authoritarianism.[30] Both theoretically and empirically, the paradigm focuses on high-level politics. It views elite politics as the politics of factionalized power struggles. Leaders gain and maintain power through a constant effort to build and strengthen covert factional networks.

2.2.1 Theory

The patronage paradigm for political selection in China takes as a point of departure the institutional weakness of authoritarianism. Formal rules,

---

[30] Some older studies of factions in Chinese politics (e.g., Pye 1980) view factions as intrinsic to Chinese culture. This older perspective is consistent with a large multidisciplinary literature on the importance of connections [关系] in Asian culture. The patronage paradigm is consistent with an inherently cultural perspective, but its dynamics derive from political structure.

including laws and regulations, lack sufficient force to constrain the behavior of those with power. The fundamental insecurity of elite politics is one result (Haber 2006). Not only is there no mechanism assuring a smooth political succession but also leaders face a constant threat of losing power to ambitious rivals (Svolik 2012; Sudduth 2017). Because they have no expectation of surviving (politically at least, perhaps even literally) a loss of power, leaders have short time horizons. Consequently, they do not prioritize supply of broadly encompassing public goods such as economic growth. Instead, they give precedence to maintaining short-term state capacity and building support from followers (Bueno de Mesquita et al. 2003; Gandhi and Przeworski 2006). Indeed, one strain in the literature, formalized in Egorov and Sonin (2011), argues that authoritarian dictators may prefer incompetent but loyal followers to shore up their relative standing and prevent rivals from staging a power grab: when loyalty is difficult to gauge ex ante, ambitious incompetent followers pose a smaller threat than ambitious competent followers do.

In China, a single Leninist-type party monopolizes politics. The ban on political parties other than the communist party and on factions within the communist party pushes all other political affiliations under the surface (Huang 2000). Although political leaders cannot compete overtly through political parties, the institutions of political selection give them the opportunity to influence the career advancement of subordinates. Career advancement is a reward that patrons exchange for the implicit promise of personal loyalty.[31] As Shih, Adolph, and Liu (2012, 169) put it: "When a factional patron comes under attack, followers remain loyal because they expect large payoffs for protecting the patron, who in turn promotes followers to the upper echelons of the regime."

Consistent with the established literature, factions in the patronage paradigm are "personalized factions" (Belloni and Beller 1978), lacking substantive ideological or policy content. As described in Pye (1981, 7) decades ago, factions in Chinese politics are "personal relationships of individuals who, operating in a hierarchical context, create linkage networks that extend upward in support of particular leaders who are, in turn, looking for followers to ensure their power." Although patrons exchange career advancement for an implicit promise of loyalty from followers in their respective factional networks, *personal* connections drive the exchange. Leaders leverage their individual endowments of personal connections to build their factions.[32]

---

[31] Political loyalty here is personal. Moreover, elite politics as a factional struggle in the sense articulated here undermines organizational loyalty.

[32] This political informality is different from corruption. Moreover, judging from bribe prices, office buying and office selling, which emerged as one of the more serious forms of corruption in

How to measure the personal connections on which factions are built? Statistical studies assume that biographical coincidences – such as shared traits or overlap in experience – are shortcuts that help patrons identify a pool of loyal followers. The patronage paradigm conventionally measures personal connections between patron and followers as one or more of the following coincidences: same province of birth, same college alma mater, or temporal overlap in workplace prior to the patron achieving high office (Meyer, Shih, and Lee 2016).[33] As discussed in Section 2.3.2, biographical coincidences such as these generate many false positives. For example, many senior officials have attended the same elite universities, such as Tsinghua University. Moreover, as Yao and Zhang (2015) point out, almost all members of the Politburo Standing Committee have worked in the same small set of provinces and big cities; consequently, defining personal connections by overlap in work experience with slightly lower-ranking officials may produce a spurious positive correlation between connections and promotion.

2.2.2 Foundational Statistical Work

Shih, Adolph, and Liu (2012) frame their study as a theoretical and empirical challenge to the claims of the tournament competition paradigm – and subsequent work on political selection accepts this framing. I discuss in this section how the main analysis of the study suffers from premise failure, but it is worth noting that it is often the only work cited to represent patronage as an alternative to some version of meritocratic selection. Different from nearly every other study, the population of interest is the party Central Committee, specifically the five Central Committees elected in 1982–2007. By investigating selection into Central Committee membership, Shih, Adolph, and Liu (2012) shift the analytical focus from subnational leaders to the country's several hundred most powerful individuals – not only in national and subnational politics but also in the state bureaucracy and the military, for example. This is useful.

Formally, as visualized in Figure 1, Central Committee members are selected by peer elites, not superiors. Every five years, at each communist party congress

---

the early 2000s, more typically involve not the leaders considered in this Element but positions where bribes are readily available: government departments in charge of public projects, regulatory agencies, and law enforcement, for example. See Manion (2015). As Burns and Wang (2010) discuss, most such cases occur at the lower level – but not all: for example, the former head of Jiangsu Province Organization Department was dismissed in 2004 for soliciting 100 million yuan in bribes from lower-ranking officials seeking promotion and former National People's Congress Vice Chairman Cheng Kejie was executed in 2000 for crimes including sale of offices. See also Zhu (2008) on the office-selling chain in Heilongjiang.

[33] Opper, Nee, and Brehm (2015) investigate this as simple "homophily" and make some effort to distinguish it from political factions.

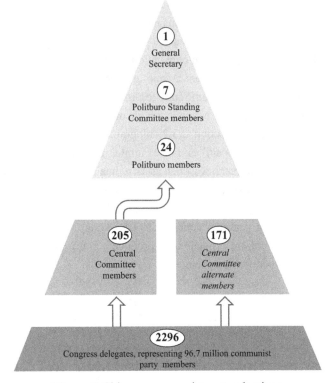

Figure 1 Chinese communist party elections

Note: Arrows indicate voting authority. Figures are for the 20th party congress, convened in October 2022.

in recent decades, roughly 2,000 congress delegates cast secret ballots to elect, in separate elections, roughly 200 full members and 170 alternate members of the Central Committee. Full members of the Central Committee then cast secret ballots to elect the Politburo, the Politburo Standing Committee, and the general secretary. The general secretary and other Politburo Standing Committee members are a subset of the full Politburo.

As with any important office in China, communist party superiors constitute the real selectorate, with powerful party incumbents managing the nomination and vetting of candidates well in advance of party congresses. Elections of the Politburo, Politburo Standing Committee, and general secretary are elections without choice: candidates on the ballots are only as many as designated offices – twenty-four or twenty-five on the full Politburo and seven on its Politburo Standing Committee in recent years. However, since the 1980s, ballots in elections for full and alternate members of the Central Committee have listed 5–11 percent more candidates than seats.[34] This presents some risk of upending personnel plans because Politburo members must first be elected as full members of the Central Committee. Indeed, a few spectacular "electoral accidents" have occurred at party congresses, with individuals designated to join the Politburo ineligible to appear subsequently on the Politburo ballot because of failure to win a Central Committee seat. Famously, for example, more than 500 delegates did not vote for Politburo-designate Deng Liqun in 1987.[35]

Shih, Adolph, and Liu (2012) argue that the Politburo Standing Committee intervenes extensively to influence the elections of full and alternate Central Committee members. The key premise of their analysis is that incumbent Politburo Standing Committee members convey to congress delegates in a variety of ways a sense of how they want them to vote for alternate and full Central Committee members – and delegates cast their secret ballots accordingly. Consequently, vote tallies reflect the preferences of top leaders. More precisely, they propose that the rank ordering of votes reflects the power and priorities of party superiors on the Politburo Standing Committee and thereby presents a metric of pecking order in Chinese officialdom. Shih, Adolph, and Liu (2012) give the label "party rank" to this metric, arguing that it reflects the distribution of latent power at the party center and thereby reflects substantive status within the communist party.

The Chinese do not report vote tallies, but they do publicize the rank ordering of votes for *alternate* Central Committee members. The centerpiece of Shih, Adolph, and Liu (2012) is a sophisticated methodology to impute from the partial observations of rank and our understanding of tiers within the Politburo,[36] using Bayesian rank likelihood modeling, the rank ordering of votes for all Central Committee members.

---

[34] Strictly, these take the form of "preliminary" elections. For the formal elections that follow soon after, the candidates with the lowest number of votes are eliminated to produce ballots that list the same number of candidates as seats.

[35] See discussion in Wu (2015, 274–277). Other examples include Xiao Yang and Yu Zengsheng in 1992 and Chen Deming in 2012. The upsets apparently greatly alarmed party superiors, who took measures to strengthen their control over the elections beginning in the mid-1990s. See Wu (2015, 277–286).

[36] Shih, Adolph, and Liu (2012) rank the party general secretary at the top, followed by Politburo Standing Committee members, followed by the vice chair and members of the Central Military Commission, followed by the Politburo members not on the Politburo Standing Committee, followed by alternate members of the Politburo. This is uncontroversial – although some might put Politburo members ahead of Central Military Commission members. The novel methodology is developed in Christopher Adolph, "Small Sample Properties of Partially Observed Rank Data Estimators" (October 6, 2011): http://faculty.washington.edu/cadolph/papers/AdolphPRDMC.pdf.

By what standard do incumbent party superiors choose whom to seat on the Central Committee? Shih, Adolph, and Liu (2012) propose that each strives to produce, as best he can, a Central Committee composed of officials loyal to him. The relevant hypothesis here among the six formulated is: all else equal, followers of top party leaders are ranked higher than other officials when their respective patrons are in power. That is, the pecking order of party rank reflects patronage connections. To test this hypothesis requires measures of presumed loyalty. Shih, Adolph, and Liu (2012) proxy this by several sorts of biographical coincidences. They draw on a remarkable dataset (described in Shih, Shan, and Liu 2010) that contains biodata for every Central Committee, with complete career histories and demographic information for each member. These data are used to test the hypothesis that "factional affiliations" determine party rank. In particular, any of three biographical overlaps is coded as a factional affiliation between party superiors on the Politburo Standing Committee and other Central Committee members: same birthplace (province), same alma mater (college), or overlap in time working at the same workplace.

Between 14 and 20 percent of members elected to Central Committees elected in 1982–2002 are concurrently subnational party or government leaders. For this subset, Shih, Adolph, and Liu (2012) also test two hypotheses that reflect the performance paradigm: as measures of relative performance, they include, as covariates in baseline models, increases in provincial GDP growth and increases in fiscal revenue.

Shih, Adolph, and Liu (2012) find no positive impact of GDP growth on party rank. Indeed, they find a "decisively negative influence" for the 1982–1997 period. For fiscal performance, they find some evidence of benefit in party rank for the Central Committee that was elected in 1992.[37] Findings on benefits of factional affiliation are also mixed. Biographical ties to Deng Xiaoping are associated with a positive and substantial boost in party rank – even for Central Committee members elected five years after Deng's death. In addition to benefits for members of the "Deng faction," they find evidence of a positive (but smaller) boost in party rank for Hu Yaobang and Hu Jintao factional affiliates.

Yet the approach in the main analysis of the study is flawed. Specifically, as noted in this section, delegates at communist party congresses thwarted arrangements of their party superiors several times in the late 1980s and early 1990s by rejecting some favored individuals in votes for Central Committee full

---

[37] It is worth noting that they visualize but hardly discuss the uncertainty around many of the estimates on the impact of performance, many of which at conventional levels of statistical significance would not reject the null of no effect. The focus on estimates rather than hypothesis testing is not uncommon for a Bayesian approach, however.

membership and thereby denying them seats on the Politburo. These are rare events but consequential for high-level politics. Upsets in elections of *alternate* Central Committee members have no such consequences, however: once they have selected appropriate candidates for the ballot, party superiors have no reason to care much about which 5–11 percent are eliminated in the election. Not surprisingly, therefore, as Lu and Ma (2019, 7) correctly observe: "There is no evidence substantiating manipulation of alternate [Central Committee] member election since 1982." This point is devastating to a Bayesian rank likelihood modeling approach that assumes electoral outcomes for full members arise from the same process as for alternate members. If votes for alternate members reflect delegate preferences, not the distribution of latent power among party superiors, then the publicized rank ordering of these votes cannot be exploited to impute a rank ordering of votes for full Central Committee members – and party rank cannot be treated as a measure of status within the communist party. In a robustness check, Shih, Adolph, and Liu (2012) address this concern by dropping information supplied by votes for alternate Central Committee members; below the five ranks at the apex of power, they simply treat full members as a tier higher than alternates.[38] Findings are roughly similar.

In their conclusion, Shih, Adolph, and Liu (2012, 183) strongly reject the performance paradigm and emphasize instead the effect of patronage connections:

> Given our findings one can no longer argue that China enjoyed spectacular growth *because* of promotion incentives embedded in the political system. . . . After the beginning of the reform, provincial administrators certainly did not have an incentive to reduce growth in their jurisdictions and may even have seen growth performance as a way to earn promotion. However, there were other (formal and informal) paths upward that were more effective. . . . First, ties with Deng Xiaoping, Hu Yaobang, or Hu Jintao while they were in power elevated officials in the party hierarchy. Even though these officials were the nominal and de facto heads of the party, they still engaged in factional politics. In fact, the literature suggests that leaders were able to stay in power *because* they engaged in factional politics instead of selecting the most capable officials.

2.3 Theoretical Revisions and Empirical Refinements

The studies reviewed in Sections 2.1 and 2.2 introduce the major contrasts in theoretical arguments and empirical findings as to the impact of economic performance and biographical connections on career advancement in China.

---

[38] See note 36 on rankings above the Central Committee. For relevant robustness results, see Figure 5 in Shih, Adolph, and Liu (2012, 180) and Appendix A.1 in the article's online appendix.

Tables 3 and 4 summarize findings on impact (positive, negative, none) from the foundational and other statistical studies on the question.[39] Both tables are organized first by level in the state hierarchy of the pool of leaders competing for promotion; for Table 4, this is the level of the client pool, with presumptive patrons one level up.[40] Why such disparate findings?

First, as is obvious from the tables, the studies analyze data for different time periods, different offices (e.g., party secretaries, governors), and even different levels of leadership (e.g., province, city, county). We do not necessarily expect similar findings across these very different circumstances. These differences have to do with *scope conditions* for theorized relationships. Second, quite apart from scope conditions are ubiquitous differences across the studies in models and measures. No two studies reported in Tables 3 and 4 reflect the same collection of choices about model specification: the models differ in functional form, in which variables are included, and in how variables are coded, for example. Sensitivity of statistical results to reasonable different specifications has to do with *robustness*. I return to these two issues in the conclusion to this section (Section 2.5). I note here, however, that the studies summarized in Tables 3 and 4, like the foundational studies reviewed in Sections 2.1 and 2.2, are mostly about effects of causes and do not take a holistic approach to explaining promotions.

My goal in this section is to sort through and illustrate notable theoretical and empirical contributions to our knowledge about political selection in China beyond the foundational work reviewed in Sections 2.1 and 2.2. All the studies reported in Tables 3 and 4 advance our cumulative knowledge about political selection in China *empirically*: they are, after all, empirical studies. Each has contributions: new data, new measures, new modeling strategies, new research designs, for example. Most contribute in more than one of these ways. All refine our knowledge of political selection, either by redefining scope conditions or by further clarifying what can (and cannot) be treated as unproblematically robust. In addition, most make some explicit *theoretical or conceptual* claim, which reflects disciplinary demands. Beyond question, some studies advance our knowledge more than others do – due, for example, to collection of a huge amount of new data (Landry, Lü, and Duan 2018), a research design that ingeniously handles the problem of causal inference (Yao and Zhang 2015),

---

[39] These constitute, to the best of my knowledge, the population of statistical studies of political selection in China published in English-language journals at the time of this writing. Some studies from book chapters are also included, but these are more difficult to track down systematically.

[40] Both patrons and clients are at the central level for the first category.

Table 3 Impact of economic performance on career advancement in China

	Statistical Study	Years	Competitors for Promotion	Impact
Province	Bo 1996	1949–1994	party secretaries + governors	negative
	Bo 2002	1949–1998	party secretaries + governors	negative
	Fisman et al. 2020	1956–2017	party secretaries + governors*	none
	Maskin, Qian, and Xu 2000	1977, 1987	party secretaries + governors*	positive
	Wong and Zeng 2018	1978–2015	party secretaries + governors	mixed
	Li and Zhou 2005	1979–1995	party secretaries + governors	positive
	Chen, Li, and Zhou 2005	1979–2002	party secretaries + governors	positive
	Opper, Nee, and Brehm 2015	1979–2011	party secretaries + governors	none
	Sheng 2022	1981–1986	party secretaries + governors	none
	Shih, Adolph, and Liu 2012	1982–1997	party secretaries + governors*	mixed
	Choi 2012	1989–2009	party secretaries + governors	positive
	Choi, Givens, and MacDonald 2021	1989–2018	party secretaries + governors	none
	Sheng 2022	1990–2002	party secretaries	none
	Sheng 2022	1990–2002	governors	positive
	Jia, Kudamatsu, and Seim 2015	1993–2009	party secretaries + governors	positive
	Hsu and Shao 2014	1993–2010	party secretaries + governors	positive

Table 3 (cont.)

Statistical Study	Years	Competitors for Promotion	Impact
Shih, Adolph, and Liu 2012	1997–2007	party secretaries + governors*	none
Landry, Lü, and Duan 2018	1999–2007	party secretaries	none
Landry, Lü, and Duan 2018	1999–2007	governors	mixed
Sheng 2022	2002–2018	party secretaries + governors	none
Chen and Kung 2019	2004–2016	provincial party secretaries	none
Chen and Kung 2019	2004–2016	governors	positive
Landry 2003	1990–2000	mayors	positive
Landry 2008	1990–2001	mayors	positive
Yao and Zhang 2015	1994–2010	party secretaries + mayors	none
Yao and Zhang 2015	1994–2010	older party secretaries + mayors	positive
Wiebe 2020a	1998–2017	mayors	none
Landry, Lü, and Duan 2018	1999–2007	party secretaries + mayors	none
Yan and Yuan 2020	2000–2017	party secretaries	positive
Yan and Yuan 2020	2000–2017	party secretaries of sub-provincial cities	none
Li et al. 2019	2003–2014	party secretaries + mayors	positive
Zeng and Wong 2021	in office 2016	party secretaries + mayors	none

Chen and Kung 2019	2004–2016	party secretaries	none
Chen and Kung 2019	2004–2016	mayors	positive
Bulman 2016	1994–2010	party secretaries: eastern provinces	positive
Bulman 2016	1994–2010	party secretaries: central provinces	none
Guo 2007	1995–2002	party secretaries + magistrates	positive
Landry, Lü, and Duan 2018	1999–2007	party secretaries + magistrates	positive
Chen and Kung 2016	1999–2008	party secretaries	positive
Zeng and Wong 2021	in office 2016	party secretaries	none
Zeng and Wong 2021	in office 2015	magistrates	positive

County

* Only provincial party secretaries and governors who are also Central Committee members.

Table 4 Impact of biographical connections on career advancement in China

Statistical Study	Years	Client Pool	Patron	Impact
Fisman et al. 2020	1956–2017	Central Committee: full	Politburo	negative
Fisman et al. 2020	1956–2017	Central Committee: alternate	Politburo	none
Meyer, Shih, and Lee 2016	1978–2018	Central Committee: alternate	general secretary	mixed
Shih, Adolph, and Liu 2012	1982–2002	Central Committee: all	Deng Xiaoping	positive
Shih, Adolph, and Liu 2012	1982–2002	Central Committee: all	general secretary	mixed
Doyon and Keller 2020	1982–2017	Central Committee: full	Politburo	none
Doyon and Keller 2020	1982–2017	Central Committee: full	Politburo Standing Committee	positive
Doyon and Keller 2020	1982–2017	Central Committee: full	general secretary	positive
Opper, Nee, and Brehm 2015	1979–2011	party secretaries + governors	Politburo Standing Committee	positive
Choi 2012	1989–2002	party secretaries	general secretary	positive
Choi 2012	1989–2009	governors	general secretary	none
Jia, Kudamatsu, and Seim 2015	1993–2009	party secretaries + governors	Politburo Standing Committee	positive
Landry, Lü, and Duan 2018	1999–2007	party secretaries + governors	general secretary	none

Center

Level	Source	Years	Position	Office	Effect
Province	Choi 2012	2002–2009	party secretaries	general secretary	none
	Opper, Nee, and Brehm 2015	1979–2011	party secretaries + governors	Politburo Standing Committee	positive
	Choi 2012	1989–2002	party secretaries	general secretary	positive
	Choi, Givens, and MacDonald 2021	1989–2002	governors	general secretary	positive
	Choi, Givens, and MacDonald 2021	2002–2012	party secretaries	general secretary	positive
	Choi, Givens, and MacDonald 2021	2002–2012	governors	general secretary	none
	Choi, Givens, and MacDonald 2021	2012–2018	party secretaries + governors	general secretary	positive
City	Landry, Lü, and Duan 2018	1999–2007	party secretaries + mayors	party secretary	none
	Yan and Yuan 2020	2000–2017	party secretaries	party secretary	positive
	Li and Manion 2023	2013–2017	party secretaries	party secretary	negative
County	Landry, Lü, and Duan 2018	1999–2007	party secretaries + magistrates	party secretary	none

or a new methodological approach (Keller 2016). The statistical studies also vary greatly in novelty.

From the studies reported in Tables 3 and 4, I select seven for review in this section. Two of them are especially interesting theoretically because they unify performance and patronage, in useful, plausible, and distinctly different ways. I select another five studies to illustrate some novel and important empirical refinements.[41] The seven studies – plus Chen, Li, and Zhou (2005) and Shih, Adolph, and Liu (2012), reviewed in Sections 2.1 and 2.2 – constitute a good "starter kit" of statistical studies of political selection in China.

2.3.1 Theoretical Revisions: Unifying Performance and Patronage

Two important studies theorize and analyze how performance and connections may work *together* (but differently) in political selection in China. These studies do not adjudicate between paradigms but unify them theoretically. The study by Landry, Lü, and Duan (2018) is also particularly ambitious: it gathers data to extend the analysis of political selection in China below the province to the city and county levels.[42]

First, Jia, Kudamatsu, and Seim (2015) borrow from standard career concern models (e.g., Holmstrom 1999) to revise performance-based models of promotion, focusing primarily on the function of personal connections in supplying information. In one story, connections *substitute* for measured performance by conveying tacit information about quality. In this formulation, leaders with *nomenklatura* authority promote connected officials because familiarity through prior experience with them gives greater confidence in the judgment that these officials have strong performance ability. This is a screening model, not a tournament competition model. In an alternative story, personal connections *complement* measured performance. In an environment where information about performance is incomplete and unreliable, connections reduce the noise. In this formulation, leaders with *nomenklatura* authority promote connected officials because these officials communicate more frequently with them and in these communications convey trustworthy information about local conditions. We can think of this as a "performance-plus" model. In both versions, whether connections deliver loyalty to patrons or not is beside the point.

---

[41] I judge the contributions in Jia, Kudamatsu, and Seim (2015) and Landry, Lü, and Duan (2018) as novel, important, or both. I also note that each of them garners significantly more Google citations than other statistical studies in Tables 3 and 4 do, with the exception of foundational studies. Distinguishing which other studies make similarly notable contributions is less obvious. The five studies I select represent a range of different sorts of high-quality empirical contributions.

[42] See also Guo (2007) and Landry (2003, 2008). A draft of Landry, Lü, and Duan (2018) was in circulation at least as early as 2014.

Empirically, Jia, Kudamatsu, and Seim (2015) work to resolve whether connections are complements or substitutes in performance-based promotion models. They introduce an interaction term (connections and GDP growth) and estimate linear probability models of promotion for provincial party and government leaders in 1993–2009. Connections are measured as shared workplace, specifically, overlap in time working in the same party or government branch of the provincial leader and any member of the Politburo Standing Committee. Performance is measured as real provincial GDP growth. Results suggest that connections and performance are complements, not substitutes. On average, connected leaders are more likely to be promoted than are unconnected ones, but the substantively large difference is driven by the stronger positive association between promotion and performance for connected leaders. That is, actual performance matters: whatever their connections, weak performers are unlikely to be promoted, although connections do increase the likelihood of promotion for strong performers.

Having concluded that performance and connections are complements, Jia, Kudamatsu, and Seim (2015) then try to assess the relative importance of connections as complements in performance-plus models and classic "coup-proofing" (Quinlivan 1999) models. In the latter, leaders build networks of clients they can mobilize in a potential power struggle. The arguments and results are ambiguous or weak, however, leaving this important issue fundamentally unresolved. The empirical strategy leverages heterogeneity in complementarity along two dimensions: differences in age between leaders with *nomenklatura* authority and connected leaders and years in office for connected leaders. First, it considers age differences between connected provincial leaders and their respective patrons on the Politburo Standing Committee. It theorizes that leaders with *nomenklatura* authority who are relatively older have greater expectations of loyalty from their connected provincial leaders but that age differences are unlikely to matter if connections mainly function to reduce noise in information. This reasoning is puzzling, however: it seems equally plausible that a smaller age difference supports the loyalty mechanism of the coup-proofing model, as patrons will be around longer, with a longer time horizon for connected leaders to consider. Second, it shows formally that economic growth becomes more accurate as a signal of ability when observed over more years. That is, longer tenure diminishes the function of connections in conveying information about performance. Results of the two analyses are inconclusive: relevant coefficients are in the predicted direction, but they are not statistically significant at conventional levels.

A more theoretically straightforward and empirically ambitious study is Landry, Lü, and Duan (2018), which builds on the tradeoff between competence and loyalty formalized by Egorov and Sonin (2011). Landry, Lü, and Duan (2018) also extend empirical analysis downward to include provincial, city, and county leaders. In this story, by design, the balance of competence and loyalty is unevenly distributed along the state hierarchy. At lower levels, meritocratic institutions privilege competence: the imperative to maintain performance legitimacy forces the party center to ensure that lower-level leaders across China deliver the economic performance necessary for popular support and regime survival. Competence has diminishing returns as leaders climb the political ladder, however. The consequences of promoting potentially disloyal leaders at lower levels are acceptable, but leaders at higher levels, many of whom also sit on the Central Committee, constitute the formal selectorate for leaders at the apex of power – and this privileges loyalty. In addition, if most lower-level leaders are indeed promoted for their greater competence, then their jurisdictional superiors are less able to distinguish them from peers on the basis of competence alone. This may make personal connections to superiors relatively more important. I return to this last point in Section 4.1.3.

To test this theorized "dualist appointment strategy" requires the additional collection of biographical data for hundreds of city leaders and thousands of county leaders, a major accomplishment. Landry, Lü, and Duan (2018) construct an original dataset for provinces, cities, and counties for 1999–2007, linking performance and connections with official careers of party and government leaders. Connections are coded in the following ways. For provincial leaders, connections with the party general secretary use a measure of workplace overlap from Meyer, Shih, and Lee (2016).[43] For city and county leaders, the provincial or city party secretaries who appointed them are their respective patrons. Several measurement choices for performance variables are especially thoughtful. First, noting that fiscal revenue is a crucial indicator of evaluation for Chinese officials (Ong 2012; Chen and Kung 2016), they estimate models with GDP growth and fiscal revenue as separate indicators of performance. The fiscal revenue measure sums up all local taxes and fees as well as shared tax revenues remitted to higher levels, but before any transfers and tax rebates received from higher levels. Second, noting that favorites may be appointed to localities that are already economically developed (see Sheng 2010), they use growth rates rather than growth levels, to mitigate concerns about endogenous promotions. Third, they capture the tournament logic of relative performance with independent variable measures that reflect the deviation of local performance from average performance of jurisdictional peers.

---

[43] They code a patron–client relationship with the party general secretary in cases where the provincial leader joined or left a workplace when the general secretary worked there at a time prior to the general secretary joining the Politburo.

Landry, Lü, and Duan (2018) estimate separate linear probability models for party and government leaders at each of the three administrative levels.[44] As noted in this section, they estimate separate models for each measure of economic performance: fiscal revenue and GDP growth. They also estimate models with and without a term interacting economic performance and political connections, to investigate the potential complementarity between performance and connections identified by Jia, Kudamatsu, and Seim (2015).[45]

The estimations yield mostly null results. An exception is the strong evidence that performance matters at the county level: the association between promotion and economic performance, however measured, for county party and government leaders is positive, robust, and statistically significant. By contrast, there is no evidence that performance improves promotion chances for provincial or city leaders. Indeed, for provincial government leaders, there is a negative correlation between GDP growth and promotion. Nor do the models yield evidence of any association of connections with promotion.[46] Overall, the results support only part of the dualist appointment logic: they support the hypothesis that economic performance has diminishing returns for performance as leaders climb the political ladder – but they do not suggest that connections open up opportunities for career advancement, either independently or as a complement to performance.

2.3.2 Empirical Refinements

Beyond the two unifying theoretical revisions reviewed in Section 2.3.1, a larger number of statistical studies offer significant empirical contributions to our understanding of political selection in China. I select five for review here. Yao and Zhang (2015) and Sheng (2022) work within the framework of the performance paradigm. Keller (2016), Doyon and Keller (2020), and Fisman et al. (2020) work within the framework of the patronage paradigm.

In an ingenious design, Yao and Zhang (2015) take as a point of departure the lateral transfer of leaders across cities. This career pattern, which, as I discuss in Section 3.2, is not uncommon in China, permits construction of a dataset that

---

[44] With a binary dependent variable, they could estimate a probit model using maximum likelihood estimation, as Jia, Kudamatsu, and Seim (2015) do, but they note that many other studies on political selection in China estimate linear models, so this allows results to be compared.

[45] Some other modeling choices have specifically to do with the addition of lower-level localities for analysis. For example, following Lü and Landry (2014), they take account of the intensity of tournament competition by controlling for the number of competing jurisdictions within the relevant higher-level jurisdiction. They also control for distance to the seat of the higher-level government to proxy political visibility.

[46] There is a large, positive, but statistically insignificant association between connections and promotions for provincial government leaders in the fiscal revenue models.

connects subsamples of cities governed by "movers" who are rotated to them at different times. Using a method developed by labor economists for linked employer–employee data, the study infers and compares "leader effects" – contributions of leader abilities to the city's economic growth – and then uses leader effects to predict promotion.[47] This is a more precise approach to estimating the effect of economic performance on promotion.

Specifically, Yao and Zhang (2015) identify a large connected subsample of 175 cities and 1,196 city party secretaries and mayors (among whom 218 are movers) for 1994–2010.[48] Owing to unavailability of promotion data, the sample for analysis is reduced to 995 leaders for 1998–2010. It is useful to note here, as Wiebe (2020b) does, that the study finds no average association between leader effects and promotion. In models that include a term interacting ability and age, the study does find leader effects, with a strong threshold effect for leaders older than fifty-one. Parsing out these results, Yao and Zhang (2015) conclude that more years of experience produce a strong signal of actual ability. Indeed, they go so far as to argue that rotation is a design feature in political selection: it allows the party center to compare leader quality within a larger number of cities.

Sheng (2022) criticizes the studies associated with the performance paradigm for their implicit assumption of an unchanging preference at the party center for higher GDP growth across all regimes (i.e., administrations, distinguished by different general party secretaries) after 1978. This assumption, he argues, is overly simple. The absolute priority of economic growth is valid for most of the Jiang Zemin regime in the 1990s. However, as shown in Zuo (2015), for example, a policy priority of social welfare under Hu Jintao in 2002–2012 changed how standards of performance evaluation for leaders were applied across China. I take up this point in Section 3.3.1. Sheng (2022) also criticizes the usual practice of aggregating the pool of party and government leaders in the same model.

Following through on this critique, Sheng (2022) analyzes the impact of economic performance on promotion of provincial party and government leaders for 1978–2018 in separate models for party secretaries and governors and for each regime.[49] More relevant for the discussion here are his measurement

---

[47] Leader abilities affect economic growth and their chances of promotion. To address this simultaneity bias, the study takes a system-of-equations approach to estimate leader effects and impacts on promotion together.

[48] Yao and Zhang (2015) assume that party secretaries and mayors contribute to city growth separately and analytically treat them as if they worked in two different but identical cities. That is, the leaders enter the analysis as two different observations.

[49] Choi, Givens, and MacDonald (2021) also theorize and find a distinction across regimes, but for patronage ties. Under Xi Jinping, the power balancing across factions observed in the Jiang

choices. Following Kung and Chen (2011), Sheng (2022) argues that accession to the Central Committee as a full or alternate member is itself a nontrivial career advancement – and he codes it as a promotion. This coding rule greatly increases the number of promotions: indeed, such cases represent nearly 43 percent of "upward moves" in the sample. When these sorts of moves accompany promotion to a more highly ranked office (e.g., a governor's promotion to party secretary), Sheng (2022) codes them as "dual promotions," assigning them more weight in his ordinal dependent variable. Whether or not this introduces a valuable correction to a serious undercounting of promotion is a substantive matter on which scholars may reasonably disagree.[50] Sheng (2022) finds no association between relative economic performance and career advancement except, as theorized, for government (not party) leaders under the Jiang regime (1990–2002).

As noted in Section 2.2, statistical studies generally rely on one or more of three sorts of biographical coincidence to identify factions in Chinese politics: same birthplace (province), same college alma mater, and overlap at the same workplace. Keller (2016) asks: Why should we expect two senior communist party officials to become allies simply because of their association with a particular province, for example? She introduces social network analysis to the investigation of Chinese factions and conceptualizes factions as strategic alliances across officials connected in an underlying social structure. Ties established through past shared experience or common background create the structure, which makes it easier for particular officials to ally with others – but alliance is a strategic choice. One of her main purposes is to evaluate which sort of overlap best captures the true underlying social structure. As the ties created by overlaps are also the most common measures of patronage connections in the literature on political selection, the evaluation is of interest here.

For analytical leverage, Keller (2016) proposes two comparisons. First, she compares ties identified through overlaps of college, workplace, and birthplace with ties identified through qualitative sleuthing by a team of journalists, which are publicly available as the Connected China database.[51] She focuses on ties connecting 166 Central Committee members in 2013. For this set of analyses, she assumes that the ties identified by the journalists are a relatively accurate reflection of a true underlying structure. She systematically searches for the ties

---

Zemin and Hu Jintao regimes has been replaced by a dominant faction. This accords with the story in Shirk (2023).

[50] At a minimum, I would prefer a distinction between alternate and full Central Committee membership, for example.

[51] Accessible at http://china.fathom.info/, compiled by a team of journalists associated with Thomson Reuters.

identified through biographical overlaps that correlate most strongly with those identified in Connected China. She also uses exponential random graph models to test whether ties that Connected China identifies between two Central Committee members are more likely when the same individuals are tied together through biographical overlaps. In a second analytical approach, she assumes that formal high office in the communist party hierarchy is correlated with informal power measured through ties created through overlaps of college, workplace, or birthplace.[52] She evaluates correlations for the Central Committees elected from 1982 through 2012. Findings from all these various efforts are highly consistent. Keller (2016, 37) concludes:

> Neither provincial origin nor university ties are particularly important in structuring elite competition and coalition formation, despite the frequent talk of such factions. It is the *coworker network* that most strongly and consistently captures the informal relationships among the Chinese political elites in the reform period. Further refinements of that network, which take into account the amount of time spent as coworkers, the number of different instances, or whether promotions have occurred during that period, increase the predictive power of the models.[53]

Keller (2016) is not making a causal claim about the impact of shared workplace experience. Rather, among the various sorts of overlap commonly studied, she finds that same alma mater or common province of birth are simply less plausible points of departure for inquiry into connections that matter. By contrast, coworker networks seem better to reflect an underlying structure that facilitates connections in informal politics, such as patronage connections.

Perhaps the best evidence that personal connections can exert a positive impact in political selection comes from Doyon and Keller (2020, 1037), a meticulous study that puts aside the usual count of college, workplace, and birthplace overlaps: "With such proxies, there is no evidence that the supposedly connected individuals even know each other." The study uses a stronger proxy. It compares pairs of alumni from three adjacent cohorts of a Central Party School year-long training program for promising young officials. The training program features intense classes, study groups, and team-building exercises – all activities likely to create personal bonds. The study's underlying assumption is that members of the same cohort, but not members of different cohorts, likely form personal bonds. The dependent variable is the usual one: promotion. The dichotomous independent variable of interest is whether or not program graduates who rise to positions powerful enough to affect promotions were in the same or a different cohort as

---

[52] Reference points are membership in four party bodies: Politburo Standing Committee, Politburo, Central Committee, and Alternate Central Committee.

[53] Emphasis added.

program graduates who are candidates for promotion. The study identifies instances where potential patrons encountered alumni of any cohort in the course of their careers and where timing was such that they could affect promotions. The analyses compare promotions of officials who share a cohort with a potential patron to promotions of officials in one of the other two cohorts.

Doyon and Keller (2020) find negligible promotion differences when potential patrons are provincial deputy party secretaries and governors. For provincial party secretaries and heads of provincial organization departments, however, the effects are large, statistically significant, and in opposite directions. Other things equal, sharing a cohort with an official who rose to become a provincial party secretary provides a big boost (25 percent, compared to 8 percent) in promotion chances; by contrast, sharing a cohort with an official who became a provincial organization department head *lowers* chances (12 percent, compared to 30 percent) of promotion greatly.[54] I discuss this interesting latter result in Section 4.1.1.

Fisman et al. (2020) analyze the impact of shared background on selection of Central Committee members to the Politburo for 1956–2017, treating incumbent Politburo members as the set of patrons. They propose and find, in their main result, a "connections penalty," which reverses the direction of the patronage relationship in most studies that adopt the paradigm. The underlying argument is that political selection into the Politburo follows a logic of distributive balance across factional networks:

> Overall, our results indicate that, at least for the highest and most visible levels of the Chinese polity, shared backgrounds may reduce the chances of promotion. ... Our work thus suggests a somewhat different view of the internal organization and promotion of China's leadership. In particular, the "connections penalty" suggests the presence of forces within the government to balance representation in the Politburo. (Fisman et al. 2020, 1754–1755)

The study begins with its preferred specification that includes fixed effects for same hometown, alma mater, and workplace. Shared hometown is measured as same city of birth, already introducing more precision than the conventional measure. Shared workplace is measured as overlap in which both potential patron and client work in the same department in the same city. They find both hometown and college ties are associated with a large, statistically significant lower probability of selection into the Politburo.[55]

---

[54] The study presents a simple *t*-test as well as analyses that control for cohort (i.e., do not treat membership in the three cohorts as exogenous) and for other individual characteristics. Results are roughly the same.

[55] For shared workplace, they find no impact, which is interesting, considering Keller (2016). They also find no direct or conditional effect of performance; provincial leaders represent only about one-fifth of the sample, however (Fisman et al. 2020, 1755, note 4).

Investigating heterogeneity in the connections penalty, Fisman et al. (2020) find it results primarily from hometown and college ties to more junior Politburo members; this is consistent with a logic of intra-group competition (see, e.g., Francois, Trebbi, and Xiao 2016), in which candidates for promotion work to gain a dominant position within a group network (i.e., same hometown or college) by blocking potential challengers from within their own group. The study also finds the connections penalty far greater under Mao, which is consistent with the relatively greater anti-factionalist concerns observed in Mao's rhetoric.

A key modeling difference between this study and studies that find connections boost promotion chances is the use of group fixed effects and the emphasis on same hometown and alma mater. Hometown, alma mater, and workplace fixed effects capture average differences in the rate of selection into the Politburo as a function of these background characteristics. As discussed in Section 2.4, Fisman et al. (2020, 1776) also reanalyze prominent existing studies that adopt the patronage paradigm.[56] This leads to the following concluding caution about model specification:

> Our main analysis and findings emphasize . . . the care required in analyzing observational data on connections. In particular, in considering the full set of potential explanations for our results, we highlight the nuanced relationship between shared backgrounds and promotion. And by comparing results based on within- versus between-group variation, we show how cross-sectional analyses may be biased toward finding a positive effect of connections when none exists.

2.4 Reanalysis of Existing Studies

As noted in Section 2.3, quite apart from the reported characteristics that reflect different scope conditions, each of the studies summarized in Tables 3 and 4 reflects a different combination of choices about model specification. Statistical studies normally include their own battery of robustness checks on a preferred model specification. We expect reasonable changes to confirm the basic robustness of findings about the relationships analyzed. This is not always the case, however – and scholars may disagree.[57] The four studies summarized in this

[56] Specifically, in Table 9 in the article, they compare their empirical strategy and results to Shih, Adolph, and Liu (2012), Jia, Kudamatsu, and Seim (2015), and Francois, Trebbi, and Xiao (2016), highlighting differences in time periods, candidate samples, patrons, types of connection, promotions analyzed, methods, and identification of connections.

[57] Robustness checks are to be distinguished from replications, which estimate the same model with the same measures for the same population, often using the same data. Replications should yield basically the same findings. Among studies discussed here, Fengming Lu, Xiao Ma, Austin

section reanalyze existing studies. The reanalysis efforts in Doyon and Keller (2020) and Fisman et al. (2020) not only refine findings in foundational studies but also offer valuable perspective on the patronage paradigm more generally. Su et al. (2012) and Wiebe (2020b) focus on particular modeling choices, which is more typical of reanalysis efforts.

Doyon and Keller (2020) update and reanalyze the data from Shih, Adolph, and Liu (2012), using probability of a Central Committee member's appointment to the Politburo in 1982–2017 as the dependent variable in a logistic regression. They define patronage connections by workplace ties: connections are established when two individuals work at the same time in the same workplace and the lower-ranked individual is promoted during that time. They find variation depends on the patron's office. Specifically, they find no effect when the patron is an ordinary Politburo member. When the patron is a Politburo Standing Committee member, the effect is positive, however. The positive effect is most pronounced when the party general secretary is patron. This calls into question the notion that connections with senior officials always help advance careers. Instead, they propose that differential effects of patronage connections on career advancement likely exist throughout the system.

In reanalyses, Fisman et al. (2020) first reproduce the central result of Shih, Adolph, and Liu (2012) and Jia, Kudamatsu, and Seim (2015), applying the original measures and estimation methods of the two studies to their new data. The key differences are due to controls for fixed effects and candidate attributes. Group fixed effects are especially decisive. They then estimate the role of shared backgrounds in promotion of Central Committee alternate members to full membership status and again find that inclusion of group fixed effects produces lower estimates for the relationship between shared background and selection: with group fixed effects, the relationship is near zero.

Su et al. (2012) update missing biographical data and correct coding errors and inconsistencies to re-estimate the models in Li and Zhou (2005) and Chen, Li, and Zhou (2005). They find no significant association between promotion and GDP growth rate and conclude that the strong association claimed in Li and Zhou (2005) and Chen, Li, and Zhou (2005) is driven by coding errors. Their changes go beyond mere corrections and replication, however. For example,

Wang, and Tusi "Undes" Wen ("Loyalty, Competence, and Personal Interests: How Do They Shape Ruling Coalition in the Chinese Communist Party," unpublished paper, May 1, 2014) replicate Shih, Adolph, and Liu (2012) as a graduate student exercise. They correct several data and coding errors but obtain largely the same results when models are rerun. In a PhD dissertation, Wiebe (2020b) replicates five studies of performance-based promotion of city leaders: Yao and Zhang (2015); Landry, Lü, and Duan (2018); Lorentzen and Lu (2018); Chen and Kung (2019); and Li et al. (2019). He concludes the results in Chen and Kung (2019) may be due to their "flawed" definition of promotion, but results for the other studies are replicable.

they adjust the coding of relative performance: rather than subtracting the immediate predecessor's moving average growth rate from the new leader's moving average growth rate, they adjust by overall national economic performance. They also recode the dependent variable – and propose a different theoretical perspective to explain China's economic development. What is relevant here is the reanalysis, which calls into question the robustness of foundational work establishing performance-based promotion for provincial leaders.

Wiebe (2020b) reanalyzes several studies to investigate the robustness of evidence for performance-based promotion: Yao and Zhang (2015), Landry, Lü, and Duan (2018), Chen and Kung (2019), and Li et al. (2019). Overall, he finds results that support a thesis of performance-based promotion of provincial and city leaders are *not* robust to his own various "reasonable specification choices" in Wiebe (2020b, 1). By contrast, evidence for performance-based promotion of *county* leaders *is* robust to these choices.

For example, Wiebe (2020b) questions the inclusion of population and inflation as covariates in models in Yao and Zhang (2015). When these variables are dropped, the effect at the age threshold for officials older than fifty-one remains statistically significant, but the average positive interaction effect of age and economic performance in the original study disappears. Questioning the models in Landry, Lü, and Duan (2018), Wiebe (2020b) observes that they estimate the effect of average performance in office after a leader leaves the post.[58] Reanalyzing the data using cumulative average growth in more conventional jurisdiction-year panel models yields consistent evidence that county leaders are promoted based on performance; the reanalysis also confirms the null findings about the effect of performance on promotion for city leaders. However, the reanalysis finds no impact of connections (or performance) on promotion for provincial leaders and a weak *negative* effect for city leaders.[59]

2.5 Conclusion

Most statistical studies on political selection in China frame their empirical work within one of two theoretical perspectives: the performance paradigm or

---

[58] Most local leaders in China do not complete their full five-year terms but instead are promoted or transferred after about three years. Landry, Lü, and Duan (2018) argue that it is, therefore, theoretically difficult to justify using performance in year $t - n$ as the key explanation for a career change at year t: because the timing of exit from a locality is unknown ex ante, leaders cannot easily time their effort strategically to maximize performance at the end of a term.

[59] Wiebe (2020b) also tests the findings in Sheng (2022) with an analysis using data from Jia, Kudamatsu, and Seim (2015). He finds no positive and statistically significant effect of performance on promotion for governors under Jiang Zemin – but his dataset is smaller, so he is only able to test for parts of the Jiang and Hu Jintao regimes. Moreover, he models and measures things differently.

the patronage paradigm. In doing so, they answer different questions about the effects of formal and informal institutions. Unsurprisingly, the last columns of Tables 3 and 4, which summarize findings of the studies, show that scholars differ in basic empirical results. Does the cumulation of statistical studies reviewed in Section 2 amount to a cumulation of knowledge?

The latter question directs attention to empirical findings – the focus of this conclusion. Yet it is useful to begin with a reminder about theory and theoretical revisions, also the subject of this section. Although starkly delineated, neither of the two dominant paradigm is implausible in theoretical fundamentals. Moreover, in the roughly ten to fifteen years since those fundamentals were first articulated and tested, scores of statistical studies on political selection have proposed small and not so small theoretical revisions – many of them moving beyond "effects of causes" approaches to more holistic approaches. Notably, Jia, Kudamatsu, and Seim (2015) and Landry, Lü, and Duan (2018) offer distinct theoretical alternatives that unify performance and patronage.

Turning to empirical findings, (how) do the statistical studies add up? On the impact of *performance* in political selection, knowledge cumulation is sizeable. Li and Zhou (2005) and Chen, Li, and Zhou (2005) support the performance paradigm in models that focus on GDP growth at the provincial level. The focus on growth makes sense, as the puzzle of China's growth motivates the studies; the focus on provincial leaders reflects limitations on available data. The two foundational studies pool data for two decades (roughly, the 1980s and 1990s) and two offices (party secretaries and governors). Subsequent statistical studies refine our beliefs about the generalizability of their findings with investigations that broaden the scope of investigation (e.g., below the province, beyond the 1980s and 1990s) and disaggregate the pool (e.g., by regime, by office). Knowledge cumulation about the impact of performance on career advancement in China is mainly the product of these efforts to refine scope conditions.

What have we learned? First, at the *provincial* level, the positive impact of performance on promotion that Li and Zhou (2005) and Chen, Li, and Zhou (2005) find does not generalize across regimes, offices, and levels of the state hierarchy. Sheng (2022) confirms a positive association of GDP growth and promotion for governors but not party secretaries in the 1990s but for neither governors nor party secretaries in the 1980s, 2000s, or 2010s. His results have reasonable substantive foundations due to changing regime priorities and division of labor.[60] Second, at the *city* level, Landry (2003, 2008) finds a positive association of GDP growth and promotion for mayors for the 1990s. Other

---

[60] Across other studies that disaggregate the data by office (e.g., Chen and Kung 2019; Choi 2012; Choi, Givens, and MacDonald 2021; Landry, Lü, and Duan 2018), there is general consensus on no impact of performance on promotion of provincial party secretaries. However, Chen and

studies that disaggregate data by office analyze the 2000s and 2010s, which effectively averages across regimes: their findings are contradictory for both mayors and party secretaries – but the preponderance of the evidence suggests no positive impact (Yao and Zhang 2015; Landry, Lü, and Duan 2018; Wiebe 2020a).[61] Finally, at the *county* level, the positive impact of GDP growth on promotion (Guo 2007; Landry, Lü, and Duan 2018; Wiebe 2020a) seems robust for both party and government leaders. This also makes substantive sense: these officials govern localities that "lie at the core of the Chinese economy and produce the critical fiscal and economic resources that the regime requires" (Landry, Lü, and Duan 2018, 8).

Even if findings on the positive impact of economic performance for party and government leaders are robustly positive *only* at the county level, we need not infer that leaders at higher levels are incompetent: those at higher levels have made it through a promotion process at lower levels, even if promotion is not always step by step.

More disaggregation of the data to refine findings is always possible and may be warranted. Yao and Zhang (2015) argue for and find an age effect. Bulman (2016) distinguishes across localities by economic development priorities. At some point, we have arrived at a different research approach, however, more "causes of effects" – and the precision may be misplaced, introducing too much heterogeneity to estimate any model, an issue taken up in Sections 3 and 4.

So far, the discussion has privileged the refinement of scope conditions in the cumulation of knowledge about political selection. The statistician George Box (1976, 792) famously wrote: "Since all models are wrong the scientist must be alert to what is importantly wrong. It is inappropriate to be concerned about mice when there are tigers abroad."[62] Adjudicating critically across models is not my purpose here. Yet, turning from the performance paradigm to the *patronage* paradigm, Box's "tigers" seem too evident to ignore. This has principally to do with the problem of measurement, which is inherently problematic.

Statistical studies conventionally infer connections from one or more of three sorts of biographical coincidences: same alma mater, same province of birth, and workplace overlap. Of these, only workplace overlap is not hugely prone to spurious findings. As Keller (2016), Doyon and Keller (2020), and Fisman et al. (2020) make scrupulously clear, it is very difficult to reliably measure connections in a meaningful way. Doyon and Keller (2020) conclude that connections

---

Kung (2019) find a positive impact for governors for 2004–2016. These studies estimate average effects across regimes, however.

[61] As discussed in Section 2.4, Wiebe (2020b) disputes the robustness of a positive association in analyses by Chen and Kung (2019) and Li et al. (2019).

[62] The better-known version of this is: "All models are wrong, some are useful."

likely have some impact on promotion throughout the system, although probably not the same impact and not necessarily positive. This is an exceedingly modest proposition, but it is justified by the problem. It is probable and intuitive that personal connections can boost chances of career advancement for anyone anywhere and perhaps more so for officials in China than for most individuals in most places. Yet the obstacles to empirical progress on this as a research question have proved effectively insurmountable. I return to this issue in Section 5.1.

3 Descriptive Challenges: Lessons from Fieldwork

Section 2 introduced statistical studies that can be fit into one or another or both of the dominant paradigms in the literature on political selection in China. It showed disparate findings even across studies adopting the same paradigm – and discussed how this typically results from dissimilar scope conditions or dissimilar model specifications. This section takes a different perspective on the disparate findings. It presents descriptive challenges from now-rich qualitative and quantitative evidence on political selection.

The evidence, much of it from fieldwork, challenges our thinking about political selection in China in two distinct ways. Most straightforwardly, it complicates statistical estimations. The age constraints described in Section 3.1 introduce omitted variable bias, the so-called lateral transfers introduce measurement error, and the various sorts of heterogeneity introduce conditionalities to the average treatment effects estimated in many statistical models reviewed in Section 2. More fundamentally, the evidence points toward a different way of thinking about how and why Chinese leaders get along and ahead in their careers. I take this up in Section 4.

The temporal, spatial, and individual heterogeneity described in this section is especially important. Already in Section 2, some studies raised this issue, pointing to variation in policy priorities by regime (Sheng 2022), variation by level of state hierarchy (Landry, Lü, and Duan 2018), and individual-level variation in evaluation standards for leaders of different age groups (Yao and Zhang 2015), for example. As I argue in Section 4, the management of these and other forms of heterogeneity is core to the process of political selection in China.

3.1 Age Constraints

After the communist party won state power on the mainland in 1949, its members became the political, bureaucratic, and military cadre corps in Beijing and across the country. They stayed in office for decades, until death or political purge. Excepting the radical years of the Cultural Revolution in the

1960s, revolutionary seniority conferred political status and higher office. This changed in the early 1980s, with the introduction of mandated age-based retirement for officials – a seemingly mundane but perhaps the most consequential of all political institutionalization projects of the post-Mao era. Although very powerful veteran revolutionaries were eased out of office only gradually, age-based retirement upended the relationship between revolutionary seniority and power in less than a decade's time (Manion 1993), as a younger and more educated cohort of leaders ascended to leadership (Lee 1991). Quite apart from this project of retirement, graduated "age ceilings," which limit eligibility for promotion at each level of the administrative hierarchy, were introduced for subnational party and government leaders in the early 1990s (Kou and Tsai 2014). Since 1997, promotions at the highest levels of politics have also tended to observe age ceilings (Miller 2012).[63]

Table 5 summarizes age ceilings and mandated retirement ages. For example, a city party secretary or mayor is eligible for promotion only up to the age of fifty-five; without a promotion, he or she faces retirement at the age of sixty. Similarly, a provincial party secretary or governor is only eligible for promotion up to the age of sixty-three; without a promotion, he or she faces retirement at

Table 5 Age constraints

	Maximum Age for Promotion Eligibility	Mandated Retirement Age
Township	40	
County	50	60 for men, 55 for women
Deputy city	52	
City	55	60
Deputy province	58	60
Province	63	65
State	67	none, but 70 and 75 observed

Notes: At lower levels, age ceilings vary slightly in regulations across localities; the ages reported here for promotion eligibility are averages (Kou and Tsai 2014). While there is no mandated age of retirement at the state level, we have observed that Politburo members beyond the age of 70 and Politburo Standing Committee members beyond the age of 75 step down, for example (Ma and Henderson 2021).

Sources: Government of the People's Republic of China (2006); Kou and Tsai (2014); Pang, Keng, and Zhong (2018); Ma and Henderson (2021).

---

[63] See Li (2022) for an argument, not convincing in my view, about observance of the age rule for the 20th Party Congress Politburo and Politburo Standing Committee.

the age of sixty-five. As for retirement, the gender difference is striking. Below the city level, mandated retirement for women is five years earlier than that for men, a practice introduced in the 1950s for ordinary state workers. The legalized age discrimination gives women less time to advance their careers. The official explanation stresses state protection of women's health, dating back to early post-revolutionary years when women entered the industrial labor force and were at the same time burdened with childcare at home.

The age constraints are a post-Mao policy intended to rejuvenate the forces of national and subnational leadership on a continuous basis. They have several implications for political selection. First and most obviously, age constraints signify that seniority is no longer a valued quality in considering leaders for promotion. Leaders are selected out (not up) on the basis of age. Unlike performance metrics, leaders cannot influence their ever-advancing age. Second, age constraints dampen performance incentives, especially as officials are rarely dismissed or demoted (Landry 2008). Kou and Tsai (2014) demonstrate the disincentive effect if the concurrent principles, which are codified in party documents, of step-by-step promotion and completion of five-year terms of office are observed: leaders will be too old for promotion to the highest level. No leader could rise above the level of deputy prefectural rank if the principles are observed. Pang, Keng, and Zhong (2018) conduct qualitative fieldwork and analyze data for city leaders serving in 1998–2012; their study confirms that age constraints and step-by-step promotion are common practices.

However, as Kou and Tsai (2014) argue and others (e.g., Landry 2003, 2008; Landry, Lü, and Duan 2018) find, stipulated completion of the five-year term before promotion is normally relaxed. Kou and Tsai (2014) show how some leaders find ingenious ways to "sprint" to higher levels. Pang, Keng, and Zhong (2018) show that a small minority of leaders are fast-tracked; by contrast, the majority, promoted on the regular track, are trapped at lower ranks until eventual retirement. The observed inverse relationship between years in office and promotion reflects the two tracks: among city party secretaries and mayors, those serving for less than three years have a greater than 70 percent likelihood of promotion; this drops to 60 percent for those serving between three and six years and to less than 50 percent for those serving over six years.[64] Zhong (2003, 122) labels these "promotable" and "terminal" tracks: "Promotable officials are those who have the possibility or expectation for promotion to higher positions or transfer to more desirable positions. Terminal officials refer to those whose

---

[64] These figures are for the bivariate analysis, but the same relationship is found in multivariate models, robustly for a variety of subsets as well as the entire sample. Forty-two percent of party secretaries and 55 percent of mayors serve terms shorter than three years.

careers have reached a dead end and who do not expect to be promoted to higher positions due primarily to age and educational background."[65]

The third implication of age constraints is broader still. Statistical models of promotion in the political selection literature customarily include a control variable (or two) for age of official. Its coefficient is normally large and statistically significant. From one perspective, this observed effect points to an extraordinary institutionalization in elite politics in China.[66] At the same time, the now requisite "control for age" when estimating effects of performance or connections on promotion introduces an important substantive point for the mechanism modeled. Age constraints are exactly that: constraints. Age constraints imply that we cannot assume that each round of evaluation is a yardstick competition between leaders at the same rank in the same subnational jurisdiction. Already, a minority of fast-tracked winners can compete to get ahead while the overwhelming majority are consigned by their age to merely get along. We cannot treat this latter group as incentivized by the prospect of promotion.[67] Further, as these "terminal" leaders do not drop out but continue for some years at the same rank, managing the economies of provinces, cities, and counties across the country, it is not quite correct to attribute the Chinese economic miracle to the incentivizing effect of political selection through tournament competition. Something else is at work. Age constraints constrain the workings of patronage connections too. At a minimum, they shrink the pool of leaders whom, due to biographical coincidence of some sort, presumptive patrons can favor with selection as reliably loyal clients.

3.2 Lateral Transfers

Chinese leaders are almost never demoted and are only rarely dismissed from office (Landry 2008). By contrast, the likelihood of lateral transfer is substantial. Lateral transfer is an appointment to a position at the same rank in the administrative hierarchy – indeed, often to exactly the same office in a different locality. For example, in 1990, Xi Jinping, then party secretary of Ningde was transferred to serve as party secretary of Fuzhou, both cities at the prefectural level.

---

[65] See also Heberer and Trappel (2013) and Smith (2009, 2013).

[66] The constitutional revision that removed term limits for the state president in 2018, which is certainly one of the more noteworthy examples of institutional backsliding under Xi Jinping, does not make these age constraints any less remarkable. More strictly relevant is the third term as party general secretary for Xi, already sixty-nine years old at the 20th party congress in 2022, which unambiguously exempts him from such constraints.

[67] Lee (2018) shows that officials who expect not to be promoted perform less well in local economic growth compared to those who are more uncertain or more confident about promotion.

Table 6 "Lateral transfers," 1996–2017

		Party	**Government**
Province	1996–2007	18.00	11.6
	2007–2017	15.8	8.8
City	1996–2007	13.6	11.0
	2007–2017	15.3	10.2
County	1996–2007	10.3	6.9
	2007–2017	10.5	5.6

Note: Figures in cells are percentages for party and government leaders in locality–year panels for the subnational levels and years indicated. For each cell, *all* career changes (i.e., promotions, transfers, dismissals, retirements, deaths) plus *no* change add up to 100%.

Source: Computed from data provided by Pierre Landry, Chinese University of Hong Kong.

Table 6 reports figures on transfers for party and government leaders of provinces, cities, and counties from 1996 through the 19th party congress in fall 2017. Although such transfers count as rare events for county magistrates, they are decidedly not so for other leaders. As shown in Table 6, the mean observed probabilities of transfer are 17, 15, and 11 percent for provincial, city, and county party secretaries, respectively. For governors and mayors, they are just over 10 and 11 percent, respectively. The substantial likelihood of lateral transfers is important for our understanding of political selection in a couple of ways.

First, lateral transfers present an unresolved problem of measurement error on the dependent variable in statistical models of political selection. Conventional coding practice in the literature treats transfers the same as no change in office. As Wong and Zeng (2018, 61) note: "The distribution of political power in China, as in many authoritarian regimes, is not fully observable." We can assume, as the literature does, that offices at a higher level of the administrative hierarchy are more politically important than those at a lower level. We can also assume, as the literature does, that party leaders are more politically important than their government counterparts within provinces, cities, and counties. The crux of the problem is that positions ranked as administratively equal, even when substantively the same office (e.g., party secretary), are not necessarily equivalent in political importance. Consider, for example, that party secretaries of Beijing and Shanghai routinely sit on the Politburo although the two megacities rank administratively equivalent to backwater provinces like Guizhou and Gansu. There can be no doubt that leaders seeking career advancement recognize such differences as ordered in political importance (and not simply a reflection of taste differences). The same is undoubtedly true of presumptive political patrons.

In short, some unknown (but plausibly substantial) proportion of lateral transfers are de facto promotions. Similarly, some promotions in administrative rank are de facto lateral transfers (or even demotions). This poses a threat to causal inference for both dominant paradigms of political selection.[68] If the measurement error is random, the resulting estimates are less precise, which affects interpretation. The evidence suggests that error is likely not random, however. In particular, some leaders are fast-tracked for promotions. Lateral transfers, which give officials a variety of experiences in training for higher-level leadership, can be integral to fast-tracking (Kou and Tsai 2014; Pang, Keng, and Zhong 2018). This implies that statistical estimates are biased.

Second, more broadly, it is worth considering lateral transfers as a design issue in political selection.[69] Just as age constraints signify what qualities are valued in political selection, lateral transfers signify what qualities the institutions are designed to incentivize. Lateral transfers curb cultivation of personal connections (strong links) within localities, but they connect transferred leaders to a greater number of other officials and localities (weak links). Lateral transfers give leaders broader experience and opportunities to excel or not – and thereby provide more information to evaluate their abilities. Additionally, lateral transfers to politically complicated sites – like Tibet or Xinjiang – can be tests of leadership (or loyalty).

3.3 Heterogeneity in Performance Evaluation

In Section 1.3, I noted some perverse outcomes of the system by which official performance is evaluated: for example, manipulation and falsification of data (Gao 2009, 2010, 2015; Li 2015; Wallace 2016). These are a product of incentives built into political selection institutions, but they are not desiderata of the party center, although top leaders are apparently aware of them. They conflict with goals of political selection institutions. This section focuses on heterogeneity in the standards by which leaders are evaluated, which is more appropriately understood as a design feature, not a flaw, of political selection

---

[68] Systematic assignment of political importance metrics is a thorny problem. Wong and Zeng (2018) make a useful first effort to construct scores for administratively equivalent localities and departments. Basically, they use proportions of officials with seats on the Central Committee as indicators of political importance. In a more recent study, Keng, Zhong, and Pang (2023) propose an index that uses the common joint appointments of party and government positions to pinpoint political significance.

[69] Yao and Zhang (2015) make a different argument but also present lateral transfers as a design issue.

institutions. Standards of performance evaluation differ across regimes and levels of the administrative hierarchy. They differ by political circumstances. Most important and least well recognized, they also differ across localities at the same administrative level in the same jurisdiction – and this presents a serious challenge to statistical modeling of promotion.

3.3.1 Different Standards across Regimes

Sheng (2022), discussed in Section 2.3.2, theorizes and shows that the assumption of the performance paradigm that growth is the top priority for every regime is too simple. Even if leaders work to best their peers in tournament-like competitions, the content of performance standards varies because regime priorities vary. Two studies take this up in greater detail, showing responses below the party center to changing regime priorities.

Zuo (2015) analyzes performance standards and their relationship to promotion under Hu Jintao (2002–2012). Her study is valuable for meticulously documenting that performance standards vary across time and place and, in particular, that standards other than economic growth achieved major importance in the 2000s. Moreover, in statistical analysis, she shows that provincial variation in calibrating performance standards to accord with the center's new policy priority is reflected in promotions below the province.

First, regimes vary. In stark contrast to his growth-obsessed predecessors, Hu elevated improvements in social welfare (e.g., education, healthcare, pensions, subsidized housing) to a prominence equal to economic growth. The change was not simply rhetorical: Beijing also expressed it in welfare-oriented performance evaluation standards in 2006, which, for the first time, also applied to leaders above the county level. Not only did the weight of social welfare indicators as a bundle increase but also several indicators (e.g., workplace safety, resource conservation, environmental protection) became imperative targets.[70]

Second, localities vary in response to regime priorities. Performance standards set out in provincial regulations reflected the regime's attention to livelihood issues to varying degrees. In almost half the new local regulations sampled, Zuo (2015) finds the overall weight of social welfare targets exceeds the weight of economic targets.[71] For example, Shandong, Shaanxi, Gansu, Hubei, Guangdong, and Yunnan provinces all assign more points to social

---

[70] Shi and Xi (2018) analyze coal mine deaths during the Hu Jintao regime and find effects consistent with relative performance evaluation and tournament competition.

[71] Zuo collects sixty-nine regulations: ten for township leaders across ten counties, forty-six for county leaders across forty-one prefectures, and thirteen for municipal leaders across eleven provinces. This is a limited, unsystematic, and unrepresentative sample – but as extensive and informative as we have in the literature.

welfare targets than to economic targets. Some provinces adapted different performance evaluation configurations to different local conditions. For example, Guangdong divided its cities into four zoning categories, with variation in content and weight of performance targets. Environmental indicators were weighted more than any others in the province's "ecological development" zones; social welfare indictors had the least weight in its "prioritized development" zones. Some provinces incentivized social policy innovation with bonuses. For example, Shaanxi awarded evaluation bonus points to pioneering practices, which led local leaders to introduce healthcare reforms that could count as a "political achievement." In Jiangxi, the top three cities in environmental protection received an annual award of US$100,000.

Li and Manion (2023) focus on the anti-corruption priority of the Xi Jinping regime and its effect on political selection decision-making below the party center. We characterize Xi's anti-corruption crackdown as a "broad purge" that has grossly exacerbated uncertainty and has raised the likelihood and cost of political error throughout the political system. One result is risk reduction in decision-making. In political selection, we theorize, leaders reduce risk by biasing promotion decisions against their own clients, to signal to Beijing that they are not building factions. Empirically, we analyze the heterogeneous impact of the purge intensity across provinces, which reflects how serious a threat the broad purge poses to provincial party secretaries who are continually making decisions to appoint city party secretaries. We find a large anti-client bias during Xi's broad purge but not for the smaller-scale anti-corruption crackdowns of previous regimes. More broadly and unlike the conventional perspective in the literature, we argue that political selection is dynamic: it responds to changing circumstances, especially political shocks.

3.3.2 Different Standards for Different Levels

As described in Section 2.3.1, Landry, Lü, and Duan (2018) theorize that what drives political selection decisions probably differs at different levels of the state hierarchy. Early statistical studies on political selection in China (e.g., Li and Zhou 2005; Chen, Li, and Zhou 2005) focused exclusively on provincial leaders; therefore, theoretical and empirical disaggregation was a moot issue. Interestingly, however, although these early studies adopted the performance paradigm, Landry, Lü, and Duan (2018) expect the balance between competence and political loyalty to be skewed toward loyalty in Beijing's decisions on provincial leaders. This is because many of them will also be elected to the Central Committee. The coup-proofing logic that underpins the patronage paradigm should not apply to lower levels, however: instead, strong economic performance in counties and townships is crucial to regime survival. Indeed, as discussed in Section 2.4, GDP growth is a robust predictor of promotions for county party and government leaders but not for leaders at provincial or city levels.[72]

A more subtle heterogeneity exists across cities that rank administratively below the province and above the county. Studies of political selection normally treat these as a single category: prefectural-level cities. Yan and Yuan (2020) study promotion paths of city party leaders but distinguish three categories: prefectural-level cities, provincial capitals, and fifteen uniquely designated sub-provincial cities. Sub-provincial cities are higher in status and enjoy greater economic authority. For example, their revenue and expenditure are directly linked to the political center, not to provincial finances. Party leaders of prefectural-level cities are ranked at the bureau level [局级]; provincial party committees have *nomenklatura* authority over them. Party leaders of China's fifteen sub-provincial cities are assigned a higher rank, however – at the sub-ministerial level [副部级].[73] The Central Organization Department has *nomenklatura* authority over them. Provincial capitals are not assigned a higher administrative status as cities, but their party leaders are also ranked at the sub-ministerial level, and the Central Organization Department also has *nomenklatura* authority over them.

Yan and Yuan (2020) find different promotion patterns for party leaders of sub-provincial cities. First, these leaders have higher chances of promotion. Second, although the cities are economically favored in various ways, economic performance does not predict promotions for their party leaders. Yan and Yuan (2020) argue that the Central Organization Department uses the party secretary positions of these cities to cultivate leaders for promotion. More generally, they argue that tournament models ignore important heterogeneity in administrative levels.

3.3.3 Different Standards for Administrative Equivalents

A more fundamental descriptive challenge to modeling political selection is heterogeneity of standards by which performance of leaders at the same level of the state hierarchy is measured. This appears in several forms. I discuss two in this section. Most obviously, at any given time, performance is evaluated with

---

[72] Of course, as discussed in Section 2.3.1, the "dualist appointment strategy" in Landry, Lü, and Duan (2018) fails in its prediction that connections drive Beijing's selection of provincial leaders.

[73] The fifteen cities with sub-provincial status are Guangzhou, Wuhan, Harbin, Shenyang, Chengdu, Nanjing, Xi'an, Changchun, Jinan, Hangzhou, Dalian, Qingdao, Shenzhen, Xiamen, and Ningbo. Ten of these cities are also provincial capitals; the analysis estimates models that take this into account with sub-sample analysis and controls. The study focuses on the career paths of party leaders, but differences in administrative rank also exist for government leaders of the three types of cities.

attention to parameters other than economic growth. Some of these parameters – social stability maintenance, for example – are extremely important in every post-Mao regime. More problematically for modeling, we can observe at any given time emphases on different performance parameters across localities at the same administrative level, even across localities in the same jurisdiction.

First, in the evaluation of "actual work achievements," performance targets are distinguished in importance as hard, soft, and imperative. Failure to meet imperative targets is most consequential because it nullifies other achievements and mechanically downgrades leaders to the "incompetent" or "unqualified" category,[74] with disastrous implications for promotion. Social stability maintenance (i.e., public order) has been an imperative target for about three decades. Its importance in career advancement is actually more axiomatic than even this designation suggests. Beijing's obsession with public order dates back to the early post-Mao years but it intensified after the spring 1989 protests. The scale of the protests caught Beijing by surprise, prompting the upgrading of social stability across the country to an imperative target (Wang and Minzner 2015). In sum, the story of post-Mao regime legitimacy based on economic performance is only partly true. Social stability has always been an extremely important parameter by which official performance is judged. For several decades, Beijing has described it not only as a necessary condition for economic growth but also of high intrinsic value. Excellent (even the top) performance in economic growth is insufficient to assure career advancement.

Secondly and less well recognized in studies of political selection, considerations of social stability and economic growth can differ in importance for careers across localities. An excellent illustration of this is the case study evidence and statistical analysis in Bulman (2016), which shows that considerations of stability and growth differ in importance for official careers across counties and provinces.

Bulman conducted his fieldwork in three pairs of counties situated directly across from one another on the shared border between Jiangsu and Anhui. The six counties are similar in geography and shared history; indeed, two of the Jiangsu counties were historically part of Anhui. Their economic conditions in the mid-1990s were roughly similar. Yet, although the three Anhui counties were on average initially wealthier than their Jiangsu counterparts, all the Jiangsu counties were much more economically successful by the time of Bulman's fieldwork in 2012–2013. Bulman (2016) finds the incentivization

---

[74] Localities vary somewhat in grading categories. In some, leaders are evaluated as excellent [优秀], qualified [合格], or unqualified [不合格]. In others, leaders are evaluated as excellent [优秀], competent [称职], basically competent [基本称职], and incompetent [不称职]. See Heberer and Trappel (2013).

and promotion story for Jiangsu is the familiar one of tournament competition, with performance in achieving economic outcomes the major influence in promotion. This is not so for Anhui, however. There, social stability dominates evaluations. "Jiangsu continues to promote its county Party secretaries on the basis of economic success. Anhui, which needs all the growth it can get, instead promotes county leaders based on stability maintenance" (Bulman 2016, 226).

Moreover, the study argues, the observed differences do not simply reflect local priorities. Extending the analysis to a national sample, Bulman (2016) finds two different promotion criteria operate in coastal and central provinces: central provinces emphasize and reward local stability in decisions on promotions, with predictable consequences for lower growth. A comparison of career trajectories of provincial party leaders suggests that regionally differentiated promotion priorities originate with the party center in Beijing. Beijing rewards leaders of wealthy coastal provinces for economic growth and rewards leaders of poorer central provinces for social stability maintenance. For example, incidents of public disorder typically doom promotions for leaders in poorer provinces, but not in richer provinces. In sum: "The center has selected some provinces to grow and reform and other provinces to maintain stability, and selected leaders reflect these emphases" (Bulman 2016, 207).

Although Bulman (2016) focuses on the two major parameters of social stability and economic growth, other parameters can take on extraordinary importance for official careers too. Even the growth priority can be reflected in different economic parameters. Xi Jinping's campaign to eradicate poverty in China by 2020 is a prime example. The campaign required a reduction in poverty to achieve a poverty incidence in each county below 2 or 3 percent, depending on region. City party and government leaders were under intense pressure to ensure that all counties nested in their respective cities exited the designation of "poor" on time. The career pressure on county leaders was the most extreme, however: the party center explicitly ruled out transfer or promotion out of the county for any county party or government leader so long as the county was designated as poor (Zhu 2022). In effect, for leaders in poor counties, reducing poverty became the single parameter that trumped all others.

3.4 Conclusion

Friedman (1966) argues that we should not fuss about realism in a model so long as it has strong predictive power, especially absent a competing model. This section fusses about realism as a response to the discrepancy in findings for the studies reviewed in Section 2. I identify several basic empirical challenges to underlying assumptions and workings of the models that produce those findings. Features such as age constraints and lateral transfers, both part of the design of political selection institutions in China, are bound to affect our statistical estimates. Heterogeneity of various sorts frustrates the modeling exercise in a more fundamental way, as conditionalities may demand too much theoretical refinement. Obviously, there are very important parameters other than growth: social stability, for example, has been a major imperative target for more than three decades. More challenging is the heterogeneity of standards of evaluation for leaders at the same level, especially those who are competing for promotion in the same jurisdiction. Section 4 proposes a perspective that is roughly consistent with a performance paradigm and inconsistent with a patronage paradigm. It puts management of heterogeneity at the center of political selection in China.

4 Views from the Inside: A "Good-Fit" Perspective

In this section, I pose and try to answer a different question from effects-of-causes studies. What do we know about how political selection works on the ground? I propose an analytical perspective that differs from the dominant paradigms reviewed in Section 2 and takes into account the descriptive challenges identified in Section 3. My main impetus is new knowledge – much of it from fieldwork and most of it conducted some ten to twenty years after the groundbreaking case studies that delineated the workings of the target responsibility system in China's townships. The key feature of the new knowledge considered in this section is not, however, its greater recentness but its various empirical efforts to get at the process of political selection from the inside – specifically, from the vantage points of two players: the leaders competing with their peers for career advancement and the party organization departments in Beijing and across China. The views from the inside undergird the alternative developed here, which I term a "good-fit" perspective.

A good-fit perspective can be considered a relatively holistic, process-focused version of a performance paradigm. Most consistent with that paradigm, it views political selection in China as highly institutionalized. It differs from the theoretical perspective described in Section 2.1, however, by identifying the management of heterogeneity as fundamental to the activities that make up political selection. As the studies reviewed here show, political selection is comprehensive, complex, and nuanced. The party center in Beijing creates rules and specifies valued qualities that give content to the various political selection activities by organization departments throughout China. The organization departments play the pivotal role in practicing institutional flexibility, with attention to spatial, temporal, and individual specificity. This on-the-ground flexibility, I argue, is integral to China's political selection institutions. Political selection is not a straightforward application of performance standards such as economic growth mandates; rather, studies show it is a nearly continuous process of selecting, from a large pool of good-enough candidates, those who are a good fit for the particular time and place as offices of leadership open up.

Political selection also notably encompasses the routine cultivation that creates this pool. These activities define the expansive delegated power of organization departments – which goes far beyond their generally recognized power, based on superior information, to vet and recommend candidates for promotion. Moreover, studies show that the power of organization departments in political selection is well-known by leaders who compete for its recognition and a favored leg-up in career advancement.

In this sense, while the perspective here shares much with the performance paradigm, it also suggests that the focus of that paradigm gets the institutional workings wrong. The application of standards in the perspective here is far from mechanical. The process is not highly legible and not focused on the single dimension of economic growth. In the good-fit perspective, organization departments are trustworthy agents of the party center, exercising broad delegated powers and professional discretion – and this is common knowledge.

The rest of Section 4 is organized as discussions of two players: organization departments and leaders seeking career advancement.

4.1 Organization Departments

Our new knowledge about organization department activity in political selection comes from a variety of sources, of which seven or eight contribute the most to the argument here. Yan (1995) is the account of an insider working in the Central Organization Department in the 1980s. Pieke (2009) documents the selection of officials for training at communist party schools, based on extensive fieldwork and interviews in 2004–2005 in Yunnan province. My own 2007–2008 fieldwork is the basis for Manion (2008, 2018), which include interviews at the organization department in Zouping county in Shandong province; Manion (2018) also consults the handwritten field notes of Michel Oksenberg, documenting more than a decade of his interviews with leaders in the same county in the late 1980s to the late 1990s. Heberer and Trappel (2013) draw on fieldwork conducted in fourteen cities and counties in eight provinces in 2007–2011. Zeng (2016) is based on fieldwork and interviews conducted in 2014 with officials in organization departments at the provincial, city, and county levels. Leng and Zuo (2022) is based on fieldwork and interviews between 2015 and 2020 with officials involved in setting evaluation targets, also at provincial, city, and county levels. Finally, Doyon and Keller (2020), the statistical study of personal connections discussed in Section 2.3.2, provide credible insight into the professionalism of organization departments.

Together, these sources reveal with new specificity the expansive power delegated to organization departments in political selection and the professionalism that makes them trustworthy agents of the party center. The characterization of political selection that emerges is a process of nearly continuous evaluation and vetting, through which organization departments accumulate abundant specific information and thereby come to really know leaders under their management. Moreover, although information may be their valuable resource in recommending candidates for promotion, as early accounts (e.g., Manion 1985) emphasize, organization departments also influence political selection by shaping the credentials of the candidate pool: for example, they choose the subset of individuals for extra cultivation at communist party schools, which effectively designates these leaders as "winners," on the fast track to fill offices as they open up.

4.1.1 Power and Professionalism

As I write elsewhere (Manion 2018), organization departments are the most powerful operational departments of communist party committees – and political selection is the crux of that power, just as it is the crux of party power in China. One measure of organization department power is the exercise of its professional duties when its most important principal disagrees on specific cases. Yan (1995) illuminates this, from his vantage point in the Central Organization Department. The essay suggests that the department does not give pro forma approval simply because a top party leader personally favors a candidate for promotion: from Yan's experience, if a leader insists on an appointment over the department's objections, the department enters its dissenting opinion into the record. In one of several examples Yan (1995) recounts, Bo Yibo and Wang Zhen recommended promotion of Chen Yuan, son of Chen Yun, to Beijing city leadership. Bo, Wang, and Chen were not simply top party leaders; they were among the "eight immortals," revolutionary elders who had led China's emergence from Cultural Revolution chaos to a new decade of post-Mao reform. The Central Organization Department objected to the recommendation, citing then General Secretary Hu Yaobang's directive that children of current leaders should not be appointed to offices at the vice-ministerial level or higher. After much debate, the Politburo resolved that Beijing's leaders would no longer be managed by the Central Organization

Department but directly by the Politburo. That the Politburo sided with Bo, Wang, and Chen (but not Hu) is not surprising. What is more interesting is how it chose to prevail: obviously, the rules change respected the "immortals" – but it also sidestepped direct conflict between professionalism and informal power. Indeed, if, as I argue in this section, organization departments have broad powers to apply highly particular local knowledge to fit candidates to offices in a heterogeneous environment of political selection, then we expect professionalism as a requisite (not merely tolerated) design condition for such delegation by the party center, the principal at the top of the hierarchy.

Apart from insight into party center intent, the example of Chen Yuan seems supportive of Yan's (1995, 47) characterization of the Central Organization Department as "strict and not factionalized." Doyon and Keller (2020) provide credible statistical evidence that substantiates this conclusion at lower levels. As reported in Section 2.3.2, they use a strong proxy for personal connections: pairs of alumni from three adjacent cohorts of a year-long training program at the Central Party School. Their study investigates whether promotions occurred for officials connected (or not) with the 8 percent of officials who rose to one of four offices of provincial leadership that offer the opportunity to practice patronage. The strongest finding is not for party or government leaders but for organization department heads: the effect of cohort connections is large, negative, and statistically significant – 12 percent versus 30 percent. Why is a personal connection in the organization department singularly unhelpful for promotion? Doyon and Keller (2020) acknowledge this as a puzzling finding but suggest organization department heads may be under relatively greater scrutiny. This is not implausible, but the finding is also consistent with Yan's (1995) observation of the relatively strict professional scruples in organization departments.

4.1.2 Comprehensive and Nearly Continuous Evaluation

The onus is on organization departments to use their information to identify high quality, so as to prevent governance failures. If they err in their recommendations to party committees, they have failed in their most important responsibility – and their failure is likely to be evident.

As described in Manion (2018), evaluation of quality takes two different forms: annual evaluations [考核] and vetting [考察]. However, the processes sometimes overlap. Both are more comprehensive than assessing whether targets are met: they are evaluations of the individual as a leader in all aspects.[75] Vetting of

---

[75] Heberer and Trappel (2013) distinguish between policy and program evaluation [目标考核] – that is, whether targets have been met – and evaluation of leaders [考评]. The evaluation of quality I describe here refers to the latter.

candidates for movement up or out occurs when an opportunity arises for a transfer or promotion, but organization departments can also use information from annual evaluation results in vetting. This puts pressure on organization departments to engage in a nearly continuous process of evaluation to identify and recommend high-quality leaders in a timely way. Nearly continuous evaluation familiarizes departments with particular qualities of leaders in the locality. It allows the departments to home in on quality so that they are prepared when specific positions open up. Organization departments routinely update and adjust their reserve pool: promising candidates to watch, cultivate, and (perhaps) recommend for appointments.

4.1.3 Deciding on Performance Standards

As noted in Section 2.4, evidence of performance-based promotion is robust at the county level but not above it. As Wiebe (2020b) reasons, if political selection institutions motivate county party and government leaders to boost local GDP growth, then leaders promoted to the city level are all high-ability leaders. Yet, if they are all high-ability leaders, there is insufficient variation in ability for a meaningful city-level tournament competition based on GDP growth. Indeed, as city officials interviewed by Leng (2018) report, they do meet the growth targets set for them. Their problem, as they describe it, is that growth does not sufficiently distinguish them from peer competitors. This leads them to seek out ways to visibly excel on other dimensions. Wiebe (2020b, 15–16) summarizes the implications for organization department work at various levels of the state hierarchy as follows: "Range restriction prevents the Organization Department from implementing meritocratic [GDP growth-based] promotion above the county level. Running a successful county-level tournament precludes prefecture [i.e., city] and provincial tournaments. Hence the Organization Department must use other criteria in determining promotions of prefecture and provincial leaders." The "other criteria" are the many dimensions elaborated in Central Committee regulations governing the selection of leaders: not only achievements and competence but also virtue, effort, and integrity. In evaluating leaders on these less easily quantifiable dimensions, organization departments are required to consult the views of a large number of other players: party discipline inspection committees, workplace subordinates, and local party members, for example (Manion 2008).

As to the easily measurable criteria, many of them are more or less endogenous. Both Heberer and Trappel (2013) and Leng and Zuo (2022) describe a process of negotiated targets that is as much bottom-up as top-down. The negotiations are highly localized and specific. They create much of the content by which leaders are evaluated. Organization departments are intermediaries in this process, working between the leaders they are charged to evaluate and the party committees with *nomenklatura* authority over them. Heberer and Trappel (2013, 1054) argue that evaluations of leaders are "an instrument of political communication" between levels of the state hierarchy: higher levels convey their policy priorities and expectations; lower levels clarify problems of implementation and their causes. Organization departments and party committees with *nomenklatura* authority do not use evaluations as punishment mechanisms, nor is it in their interest to set lower levels up for failure. As Leng and Zuo (2022) note, if assigned targets are too high, lower levels will fail or falsify data – both of which constitute failed outcomes.

4.1.4 Cultivation of Talent

Doyon and Keller (2020), discussed in Section 2.3.2, analyze cohort effects for officials who undergo a year-long training program at the Central Party School. Party schools exist below the political center, at every level of the state hierarchy. The training programs are core to the cultivation of talent. Organization departments select officials for the programs and also consult with party school leaders on content of training (Pieke 2009; Lee 2013, 2015; Manion 2018; Pang, Keng, and Zhong 2018). As noted in Section 3.1, Pang, Keng, and Zhong (2018) document two career tracks: a fast track for "preferred" leaders and a regular track for others. The same study analyzes the impact of party school training on career track. It finds training is significantly associated with shorter terms and faster promotions. That is, a subset of leaders is selected early (by organization departments) for cultivation and promoted more quickly to avoid coming up against age constraints.

In this way, organization departments give some leaders a leg-up in career advancement, advantaging them with privileged cultivation. As described in Pieke (2009, 193) and consistent with the account in Doyon and Keller (2020), party school training programs are "an item of conspicuous consumption, ... reinforcing [a] sense of being special and privileged." At the same time, the massive investment in party schools has produced a corps of leaders who are "incomparable to their predecessors of twenty years ago in terms of their educational qualifications, managerial skills and understanding of China and the world."

4.2 Leaders Getting Along and Ahead

Turning to the officials who are candidates (or not) for appointments and promotions, our new knowledge includes findings from qualitative fieldwork interviews as well as surveys. The account in Landry (2008) analyzes data from a probability sample survey of 245 officials who are heads and deputy heads of county government departments in Jiangsu. Boittin, Distelhorst, and Fukuyama (2016) present findings from a survey of 2,575 officials in 56 departments in 4 purposively selected Chinese cities. These are the two studies that most directly address the key questions for this section. In addition, as noted in Section 4.1.4, Pieke (2009) presents findings based on fieldwork and interviews in party schools in Yunnan province in the early 2000s. Ma, Tang, and Yan (2015) present findings from a convenience sample of 886 mostly grassroots officials. Finally, Pang, Keng, and Zhong (2018) present findings from interviews with forty-five middle-ranking and low-ranking officials. It is worth noting that these studies do not feature as survey respondents or interview subjects the leaders defined in Section 1.2 as the population of interest here. Therefore, we can only speculate about generalizability beyond the officials surveyed or interviewed.

4.2.1 Organization Department Power

The main argument about the importance of organization departments focuses on their broad delegated power. Two studies that focus on what Chinese officials believe about political selection conclude that officials recognize this power.

First, qualitative evidence comes from interviews in Pieke (2009). Officials spontaneously offer this view about organization department power. For example, when asked about his future plans, one official comments: "There is little point in thinking about that. You just put all your energy in the actual job you have to do and gain the support from the masses and recognition from the organization department. As for the issue of promotion, that is decided by the organization department" (Pieke 2009, 158).

Second, Landry (2008) reports statistical evidence from original survey data. A survey item asks how important specified leaders and organizations (e.g., party secretaries, discipline inspection committees) at specified administrative levels are for promotions of officials "at your level." Results show that officials know exactly which organization department (i.e., at which level of the state hierarchy) is associated with *nomenklatura* authority over them. Further, officials see differences in the importance of leaders and organizations in predicting the probability of promotion for officials like them – and they recognize organization departments as the most important. More than 86 percent named organization departments as the most important, compared to 77 percent for the party committees that have formal decision-making authority in their appointments and promotions. Party secretaries are perceived as roughly equal in importance to organization departments in determining promotions.

4.2.2 Meritocratic Promotion

Whether leaders widely subscribe to the perspective described in the patronage paradigm or the performance paradigm has obvious implications for the party as an organization. This applies to leaders selected to get ahead and, more importantly perhaps, those consigned to merely get along. Promotions are rare events. Considering age constraints, successful leaders cannot expect more than three or four major promotions in the course of a career. As Landry (2008, 119) puts it: "Assuming that the distant future is heavily discounted, disgruntled agents have few incentives to keep cooperating with their principals. If expected promotions do not materialize, they may conclude that continued defection (shirking) is the best course of action because opportunities for repeated play are limited." That is, expectations of performance-based promotion are incentivizing. By contrast, views that career advancement is based on patronage and connections can be seriously dysfunctional for the party as an organization.

Boittin, Distelhorst, and Fukuyama (2016) report on an original survey organized around questions of meritocratic recruitment, individual autonomy, and bureaucratic morale. The questions most relevant here ask officials to rate their agreement or disagreement with statements about recruitment ("My workplace is able to recruit individuals with suitable skills") and promotion ("Promotions in my work unit are based on merit"). Their main interest is comparison with officials in US federal government departments. They use statistical measures to identify and drop respondents with notable social desirability bias. They find the Chinese officials, compared to the American officials, view recruitment and promotion as significantly more meritocratic. The most dramatic difference is in response to the question about meritocratic recruitment: even after entropy balancing on respondent gender, age, supervisory status, experience in government, and education, the mean response of Chinese officials exceeds that of US federal officials by 0.63 to 0.70 on a five-point Likert scale. These are surprising findings.

Ma, Tang, and Yan (2015) also survey officials on their beliefs about promotion. Respondents are asked to check all factors they believe determine promotion for Chinese officials. Forty percent respond that promotion is solely merit-based (i.e., based on work competence or performance or both), 19 percent respond it is solely based on connections, and 9 percent respond that it is both merit-based and connections-based.[76] In multivariate analyses, the respondent's rank is positively associated with the view of promotion as merit-based. Age is negatively

---

[76] Thirty-one percent have other responses that are not easily categorized: intentions of the core leader, personnel management institutions, for example.

associated with this view. Considering the survey methodology and the relatively low rank of surveyed officials, we cannot make too much of these findings beyond the respondents. Descriptively, it is worth noting that neither paradigm dominates beliefs, although "merit only" responses are double those ascribing promotion to connections only. Unsurprisingly, promotion "winners" tend more to ascribe promotion to merit. The negative association of age with views that selection is meritocratic is consistent with the discussion in Section 3.1: age constraints greatly affect those who are not fast-tracked for advancement.

4.3 Conclusion

The perspective presented in this section puts one player at the center of our attention and makes specificity a general rule. The party center in Beijing designs, propagates, and regularly updates the content of its political selection institutions – but the key player in political selection activities is the organization departments. These departments, which are today, as in decades past, the most powerful among the party's departments, have a more difficult role than ever: making political selection work, guided by Beijing's rules but more essentially through continuous evaluation that allows them to know the candidates under their management well so that they are always ready to place them. As noted in Section 4.1.1, Yan (1995) argues, as an insider, that the departments are agents of the party center in exercising the broad discretionary authority delegated to them. This view is supported by Doyon and Keller (2020), who show that personal connections in the powerful organization departments are unhelpful to officials striving to get ahead.

A perspective that puts heterogeneity at its core, as I do here, does not lend itself well to testing, although it may help explain why findings in the existing literature are so much at odds. It is not, however, a rejection of any overarching paradigm. It sees the political selection process as institutionalized but highly nuanced. Organization departments are crucial players in ways that go beyond the mechanical application of well-articulated standards in evaluating performance. Such a mechanical view both underestimates the department's delegated authority and overestimates the legibility of their assignment. It also misconstrues the process, which is comprehensive and nearly continuous.

5 Conclusion

My aim in this Element has been to structure our knowledge about political selection in China, with a review and rethinking of foundations and findings in statistical studies as well as qualitative fieldwork-based studies. In this Conclusion,

I briefly summarize my perspective on the two paradigms that dominate research on this important question. I consider the broad questions that inspire each research project: the political economy of China's growth and the degree to which China's elite politics is institutionalized. I then turn to changes over the past decade under Xi Jinping and reflect on their relationship to political selection. I conclude by circling back to the ideas in the opening paragraph of this Element – thinking through implications of changes under Xi for the view of political selection in China as a "successful contrast" to political selection in liberal democracies.

5.1 Assessing Dominant Paradigms

The *patronage paradigm* for political selection builds on an insight into the informational deficit of China's authoritarian politics. Leninist organizational discipline bans party factions. It demands communist party loyalty to the ideas and individuals at the apex of the party hierarchy in Beijing. Alternatives to the all-party aggregation of preferences for policies or people are politically risky, even gravely punishable. As a result, pronouncements of loyalty are not credible. Unlike, for example, a politician's party membership in liberal democracies, such pronouncements convey no information to principals or anyone. In the patronage paradigm, party superiors use their authority over political selection to build networks of clients, whose loyalty can presumably be counted on in a power struggle.

On average, it is not unreasonable to presume that connections can offer strivers a leg-up on the career ladder in China. The key challenge to patronage as a research paradigm is a function of its core insight: just as would-be patrons have difficulty identifying clients whose loyalty can be presumed, so too do researchers have difficulty identifying patron–client factions. Proponents of the paradigm look to biographical coincidences for markers that may bind higher and lower officials together: same alma mater, same birthplace, or overlap in workplace experience. Yet these markers overidentify potential factions and are prone to produce spurious results. As I conclude in Section 2.5, the measurement problem for patronage models is serious and fundamental.

In an important contribution to the consideration of patronage, Jiang (2018) turns this problem upside down: political selection decisions are the source (not outcome) of patronage relationships. Party superiors use their *nomenklatura* authority to accrue clients through appointments and promotions in the jurisdictions they manage. This conceptualization of factions is highly appealing, not least of all because the patron–client relationship is the result of observable high-stakes choices, not biographical endowments. Of course, in this framing, political selection decisions like promotions are a point of departure, not the research question being investigated.

The *performance paradigm* rests on a different basic insight: the Chinese state is unusually structured so that the borders delineating equivalently self-contained localities also define a hierarchy of administrative ranks, which permits competition for career advancement to be structured as a tournament between leaders in each locality. Yet this is complicated by design features that are integral to political selection. Mandated age-based retirement and graduated "age ceilings" that limit eligibility for promotion suggest that a tournament competition model is too simple. Some leaders can compete with peers to get ahead but most face age constraints and can only aspire to get along. We cannot treat age-constrained leaders as incentivized by the prospect of promotion. Moreover, managing well the vast heterogeneous "pieces" of China requires attention to important parameters other than growth. If we accept the relevance to political selection of heterogeneity across localities at the same level, even localities in the same jurisdiction, then we should not expect the performance paradigm to predict very well.

5.2 Political Selection and Economic Growth

In tournament competition across leaders in the same locality, do better economic growth performers advance? At the county level, the evidence suggests that, on average, they do. At higher levels, top growth performance matters less for career advancement. The evidence considered in this Element suggests that political selection in China indeed contributes to China's economic growth but not exactly as the performance paradigm conjectures. Growth performance is not unrewarded: leaders in the large pool of candidates that organization departments cultivate generally meet a threshold of good-enough economic performance.

Promoting the best GDP growth performer would likely be the simplest decision rule of political selection. Yet growth performance fails to distinguish sufficiently across leaders, which poses an incentive problem for leaders and a selection problem for the communist party. This may be more crucial at higher levels of the state hierarchy, where competition is fiercer. Certainly, at higher levels, organization departments have access to relatively more information about the effort and talent of leaders under their management, as a straightforward mechanical effect: leaders who have advanced up the hierarchy have normally had longer and more varied careers than leaders at lower levels. Political selection at higher levels can, is, and perhaps must be more informationally complicated and comprehensive.

Unquestionably, however, the formal institutions of political selection that the party center in Beijing introduced in the 1980s link career advancement of leaders to a system of regularly assessed performance on many dimensions that reflect Beijing's policy priorities. Economic performance, particularly growth, has been a priority for every post-Mao regime, although not always the top priority. Across China, researchers find growth weighted heavily in all actual examples of performance evaluation tables. Moreover, growth is relatively easily measured. Its informational demands are low. For the ruling party as an organization, rewarding growth also has the merit of boosting performance legitimacy. Even if not all leaders are similarly motivated to promote growth, political selection institutions have created an organizational culture of performance, which, in most regimes in China's post-Mao era, translates into an organizational culture of growth.

5.3 Political Selection as Institutionalized?

To what extent should we characterize political selection in China as institutionalized? I focus in this Element on selection of leaders of provinces, cities, and counties, which is also the focus of most of the literature. My own perspective is consistent with the performance paradigm in the view that it is highly institutionalized. An obvious point of departure is the formal system introduced and elaborated beginning in the early 1980s, as part of the larger project of institution building that followed the Cultural Revolution. Section 1.3 described that system, which gives more structure and detail to the decades-old *nomenklatura* authority of party committees. There is also no question that the party center has continually articulated the qualities it values, which give highly specific content to the metrics that provincial, city, and county party committees and their organization departments use in evaluating performance and to actual appointments and promotions. In Section 4, I argue that organization departments practice on-the-ground institutional flexibility in political selection: from the population of possible candidates for promotion, they cultivate large pools of good-enough candidates; then, in a nearly continuous process that is attentive to spatial, temporal, and individual specificity, they select the ones who are a good fit as offices open up. This management of heterogeneity is fundamental to the activities of political selection. It does not preclude a perspective of political selection as institutionalized.

What to make, then, of the outcomes at the highest level of political selection we observed at the 20th party congress in 2022? On the one hand, by virtue of having risen through the ranks of the system described in Section 1.3, Xi's six colleagues on the Politburo Standing Committee are well qualified for high leadership: all in their sixties, they are experienced, educated, and have proved themselves competent. These outcomes reflect China's political selection institutions at work, over decades – and they present an example, at the highest level, of the success that draws attention to China as a successful contrast to liberal democratic versions of political selection. At the same time, unlike any party leader since Mao Zedong and yet to the surprise of no one, the party congress concluded with Xi still at the top of the political hierarchy after ten years in power. The men on the Politburo Standing Committee are all "Xi's men," selected from a large pool of leaders with a biographical connection to him, a lack of balance that breaks with the practice of previous post-Mao regimes. Nor did these highest-level appointments at the congress point to an elite agreement on succession to Xi, also unlike previous regimes.

More broadly, at the apex of power in Beijing, decision makers have no higher-level designer or enforcer of rules. At this highest-level elite politics, what we have conceptualized as the march of institutionalization since the 1980s has always, at base, consisted of choices by a few men to observe nascent continuities as one general party secretary follows another. These men can choose to flout precedent, however – as we observe over the past decade of the Xi Jinping regime. Xi has broken with practices of his recent predecessors, including practices directly relevant and important to political selection at the highest levels. That one man can leverage his power to realize the collection of outcomes we observe at the 20th party congress illustrates the limits of political selection institutions under authoritarianism.

References

Ang, Yuen Yuen. 2016. *How China Escaped the Poverty Trap*. Cornell Studies in Political Economy. Ithaca, NY: Cornell University Press.

Balla, Steven J., and William T. Gormley Jr. 2017. *Bureaucracy and Democracy: Accountability and Performance*. 4th ed. Thousand Oaks, CA: CQ Press.

Barnett, A. Doak. 1967. *Cadres, Bureaucracy, and Political Power in Communist China*. New York: Columbia University Press.

Bell, Daniel A. 2015. *The China Model: Political Meritocracy and the Limits of Democracy*. Princeton, NJ: Princeton University Press.

Belloni, Dennis C., and Frank P. Beller. 1978. "Party and Faction: Modes of Political Competition." In *Faction Politics: Political Parties and Factionalism in Comparative Perspective*, edited by Dennis C. Belloni and Frank P. Beller, 417–450. Santa Barbara, CA: ABC-Clio.

Besley, Timothy. 2005. "Political Selection." *Journal of Economic Perspectives*, vol. 19, no. 3: 43–60.

Besley, Timothy, and Marta Reynal-Querol. 2011. "Do Democracies Select More Educated Leaders?" *American Political Science Review*, vol. 105, no. 3: 552–566.

Bo, Zhiyue. 1996. "Economic Performance and Political Mobility: Chinese Provincial Leaders." *Journal of Contemporary China*, vol. 5, no. 12: 135–154.

Bo, Zhiyue. 2002. *Chinese Provincial Leaders: Economic Performance and Political Mobility since 1949*. Armonk, NY: M. E. Sharpe.

Boittin, Margaret, Greg Distelhorst, and Francis Fukuyama. 2016. "Reassessing the Quality of Government in China." MIT Sloan Research Paper No. 5181-16, MIT Political Science Department Research Paper No. 2016-38. SSRN. http://dx.doi.org/10.2139/ssrn.2875244.

Box, George E. P. 1976. "Science and Statistics." *Journal of the American Statistical Association*, vol. 71, no. 356: 791–799.

Brehm, John, and Scott Gates. 1997. *Working, Shirking, and Sabotage: Bureaucratic Response to a Democratic Public*. Ann Arbor: University of Michigan Press.

Brødsgaard, Kjeld Erik. 2004. "Management of Party Cadres in China." In *Bringing the Party Back In: How China Is Governed*, edited by Kjeld Erik Brodsgaard and Zheng Yongnian, 57–91. Singapore: Eastern Universities Press.

Buchanan, James M. 1989. *Essays on the Political Economy.* Honolulu: University of Hawaii Press.

Bueno de Mesquita, Bruce, Alastair Smith, Randolph M. Siverson, and James D. Morrow. 2003. *The Logic of Political Survival.* Cambridge, MA: MIT Press.

Bulman, David. 2016. *Incentivized Development in China: Leaders, Governance, and Growth in China's Counties.* Cambridge: Cambridge University Press.

Burns, John P. 1989. *The Chinese Communist Party's Nomenklatura System.* Armonk, NY: M. E. Sharpe.

Burns, John P. 1994. "Strengthening Central CCP Control of Leadership Selection: The 1990 Nomenklatura." *China Quarterly*, no. 138: 458–491.

Burns, John P. 2006. "The Chinese Communist Party's Nomenklatura System As a Leadership Selection Mechanism: An Evaluation." In *The Chinese Communist Party in Reform*, edited by Kjeld Erik Brodsgaard and Zheng Yongnian, 33–59. London: Routledge.

Burns, John P., and Xiaoqi Wang. 2010. "Civil Service Reform in China: Impacts on Civil Servants' Behaviour." *China Quarterly*, no. 201: 58–78.

Carey, John M. 2000. "Parchment, Equilibria, and Institutions." *Comparative Political Studies*, vol. 33, nos. 6 and 7: 735–761.

Chaffee, John W. 1995. *The Thorny Gates of Learning in Sung China.* Albany: State University of New York Press.

Chan, Hon S. 2004. "Cadre Personnel Management in China: The Nomenklatura System, 1990–1998." *China Quarterly*, no. 179: 703–734.

Chan, Hon S., and Jie Gao. 2008. "Performance Measurement in Chinese Local Governments." *Chinese Law and Government*, vol. 41, nos. 2–3: 4–9.

Chandler, Alfred D. 1962. *Strategy and Structure: Chapters in the History of the Industrial Enterprise.* Cambridge, MA: MIT Press.

Chen, Ting, and James K.-S. Kung. 2016. "Do Land Revenue Windfalls Create a Political Resource Curse? Evidence from China." *Journal of Development Economics*, vol. 123: 86–106.

Chen, Ting, and James K.-S. Kung. 2019. "Busting the Princelings: The Campaign against Corruption in China's Primary Land Market." *Quarterly Journal of Economics*, vol. 134, no. 1: 185–226.

Chen, Ye, Hongbin Li, and Li-An Zhou. 2005. "Relative Performance Evaluation and the Turnover of Provincial Leaders in China." *Economics Letters*, vol. 88, no. 3: 421–425.

Choi, Eun Kyong. 2012. "Patronage and Performance: Factors in the Political Mobility of Provincial Leaders in Post-Deng China." *China Quarterly*, no. 212: 965–981.

Choi, Eun Kyong, John Wagner Givens, and Andrew MacDonald. 2021. "From Power Balance to Dominant Faction in Xi Jinping's China." *China Quarterly*, no. 248: 935–956.

De Weerdt, Hilde. 2007. *Competition over Content: Negotiating Standards for the Civil Service Examinations in Imperial China (1127–1279)*. Cambridge, MA: Harvard University Asia Center.

Dittmer, Lowell. 1995. "Chinese Informal Politics." *China Journal*, no. 34: 1–39.

Donnithorne, Audrey. 1972. "China's Cellular Economy: Some Economic Trends since the Cultural Revolution." *China Quarterly*, no. 52: 605–619.

Doyon, Jerome, and Franziska Barbara Keller. 2020. "Knowing the Wrong Cadre? Networks and Promotions in the Chinese Party-State." *Political Studies*, vol. 68, no. 4: 1036–1053.

Edin, Maria. 1998. "Why Do Chinese Local Cadres Promote Growth? Institutional Incentives and Constraints of Local Cadres." *Forum for Development Studies*, no. 1: 97–127.

Edin, Maria. 2003. "State Capacity and Local Agent Control in China: CCP Cadre Management from a Township Perspective." *China Quarterly*, no. 173: 35–52.

Egorov, Georgy, and Konstantin Sonin. 2011. "Dictators and Their Viziers: Endogenizing the Loyalty–Competence Tradeoff." *Journal of the European Economic Association*, vol. 9, no. 5: 903–930.

Elman, Benjamin A. 2000. *A Cultural History of Civil Examinations in Late Imperial China*. Berkeley: University of California Press.

Fiorina, Morris P. 1981. *Retrospective Voting in American National Elections*. New Haven, CT: Yale University Press.

Fisman, Raymond, Jing Shi, Yongxiang Wang, and Weixing Wu. 2020. "Social Ties and the Selection of China's Political Elite." *American Economic Review*, vol. 110, no. 6: 1752–1781.

Francois, Patrick, Francesco Trebbi, and Kairong Xiao. 2016. "Factions in Nondemocracies: Theory and Evidence from the Chinese Communist Party." NBER Working Paper No. 22775. www.nber.org/system/files/working_papers/w22775/w22775.pdf.

Friedman, Milton. 1966. "The Methodology of Positive Economics." In *Essays in Positive Economics*, edited by Milton Friedman, 3–16, 30–43. Chicago, IL: University of Chicago Press.

Gailmard, Sean. 2002. "Expertise, Subversion, and Bureaucratic Discretion." *Journal of Law, Economics, and Organization*, vol. 18, no. 2: 536–555.

Gandhi, Jennifer, and Adam Przeworski. 2006. "Authoritarian Institutions and the Survival of Autocrats." *Comparative Political Studies*, vol. 40, no. 11: 1279–1301.

Gao, Jie. 2009. "Governing by Goals and Numbers: A Case Study in the Use of Performance Measurement to Build State Capacity in China." *Public Administration and Development*, vol. 29, no. 1: 21–31.

Gao, Jie. 2010. "Hitting the Target but Missing the Point: The Rise of Non-Mission-Based Targets in Performance Measurement of Chinese Local Governments." *Administration and Society*, vol. 42, no. 1: 56–76.

Gao, Jie. 2015. "Pernicious Manipulation of Performance Measures in China's Cadre Evaluation System." *China Quarterly*, no. 223: 618–637.

Government of the People's Republic of China. 2006. *Regulations on Retirement for Officials* [老干部离休退休的年龄规定]. National Food and Strategic Reserves Administration, April 29. www.lswz.gov.cn/html/sjzz/gbbgs/2018-06/14/content_235867.shtml#:~:text=%E6%8C%89%E7%85%A7%E5%85%9A%E5%92%8C%E5%9B%BD%E5%AE%B6%E7%8E%B0%E8%A1%8C,%E5%A5%B3%E5%B9%B4%E6%BB%A155%E5%91%A8%E5%B2%81%E3%80%82.

Guo, Gang. 2007. "Retrospective Economic Accountability under Authoritarianism: Evidence from China." *Political Research Quarterly*, vol. 60, no. 3: 378–390.

Haber, Stephen. 2006. "Authoritarian Government." In *The Oxford Handbook of Political Economy*, edited by Barry R. Weingast and Donald A. Wittman, 693–707. Oxford: Oxford University Press.

Hazan, Reuven Y., and Gideon Rahat. 2010. *Democracy within Parties: Candidate Selection Methods and Their Political Consequences*. Oxford: Oxford University Press.

Heberer, Thomas, and Rene Trappel. 2013. "Evaluation Processes, Local Cadres' Behavior and Local Development Processes." *Journal of Contemporary China*, vol. 22, no. 84: 1048–1066.

Herbert, Penelope A. 1988. *Examine the Honest, Appraise the Able: Contemporary Assessments of Civil Service Selection in Early T'ang China*. Canberra: Australian National University Press.

Holmstrom, Bengt. 1999. "Managerial Incentive Problems: A Dynamic Perspective." *Review of Economic Studies*, vol. 66, no. 1: 169–182.

Hsu, S. Philip, and Jhih-Wei Shao. 2014. "The Rule-Bound Personnel Turnover of China's Provincial Leaders, 1993–2010." In *Choosing China's Leaders*, edited by Chien-wen Kou and Xiaowei Zang, 97–123. London: Routledge.

Huang, Jing. 2000. *Factionalism in Chinese Communist Politics*. Cambridge Modern China Series. Cambridge: Cambridge University Press.

Huang, Yasheng. 1995. "Administrative Monitoring in China." *China Quarterly*, no. 143: 828–843.

Jia, Ruixue, Masayuki Kudamatsu, and David Seim. 2015. "Political Selection in China: The Complementary Roles of Connections and Performance." *Journal of the European Economic Association*, vol. 13, no. 4: 631–668.

Jiang, Junyan. 2018. "Making Bureaucracy Work: Patronage Networks, Performance Incentives, and Economic Development in China." *American Journal of Political Science*, vol. 62, no. 4: 982–999.

Keefer, Philip, and Stephen Knack. 1997. "Why Don't Poor Countries Catch Up? A Cross-National Test of an Institutional Explanation." *Economic Inquiry*, vol. 25, no. 3: 590–602.

Keller, Franziska Barbara. 2016. "Moving beyond Factions: Using Social Network Analysis to Uncover Patronage Networks among Chinese Elites." *Journal of East Asian Studies*, vol. 16, no. 1: 17–41.

Keng, Shu, Lingna Zhong, and Baoqing Pang. 2023. "Pinpointing the Chinese Nomenklatura: An Index to Rank China's Leadership Positions." *Journal of Contemporary China*, vol. 32, no. 141: 510–523.

Key, V. O. 1966. *The Responsible Electorate: Rationality in Presidential Voting, 1936–1960.* Cambridge, MA: Belknap Press of Harvard University Press.

Kou, Chien-Wen, and Wen-Hsuan Tsai. 2014. "'Sprinting with Small Steps' towards Promotion: Solutions for the Age Dilemma in the CCP Cadre Appointment System." *China Journal*, no. 71: 153–171.

Krugman, Paul. 1993. "How I Work." *American Economist*, vol. 37, no. 2: 25–31.

Kung, James, and Shuo Chen. 2011. "The Tragedy of the Nomenklatura: Career Incentives and Political Radicalism during China's Great Leap Famine." *American Political Science Review*, vol. 105, no. 1: 27–45.

Lam, Tao-chiu, and Hon S. Chan. 1996. "Reforming China's Cadre Management System: Two Views of a Civil Service." *Asian Survey*, vol. 36, no. 8: 772–786.

Landry, Pierre F. 2003. "The Political Management of Mayors in Post-Deng China." *Copenhagen Journal of Asian Studies*, no. 17: 31–58.

Landry, Pierre F. 2008. *Decentralized Authoritarianism in China: The Communist Party's Control of Local Elites in the Post-Mao Era.* Cambridge: Cambridge University Press.

Landry, Pierre F., Xiaobo Lü, and Haiyan Duan. 2018. "Does Performance Matter? Evaluating Political Selection along the Chinese Administrative Ladder." *Comparative Political Studies*, vol. 51, no. 8: 1074–1105.

Lee, Charlotte. 2013. "Party Selection of Officials in Contemporary China." *Studies in Comparative International Development*, vol. 48, no. 3: 356–379.

Lee, Charlotte. 2015. *Training the Party: Party Adaptation and Elite Training in Reform-Era China.* Cambridge: Cambridge University Press.

Lee, Hong Yung. 1991. *From Revolutionary Cadres to Party Technocrats in Socialist China*. Berkeley: University of California Press.

Lee, Jonghyuk. 2018. "Band of Rivals: Career Incentives, Elite Competition, and Economic Growth in China." SSRN. https://papers.ssrn.com/sol3/papers .cfm?abstract_id=3416118.

Leng, Ning. 2018. "Visible Development First: The Political Economy of Restructuring China's Public Service Sectors." PhD dissertation, University of Wisconsin–Madison.

Leng, Ning, and Cai (Vera) Zuo. 2022. "Tournament-Style Bargaining within Boundaries: Setting Targets in China's Cadre Evaluation System." *Journal of Contemporary China*, vol. 31, no. 133: 116–135.

Li, Hongbin, and Li-An Zhou. 2005. "Political Turnover and Economic Performance: The Incentive Role of Personnel Control in China." *Journal of Public Economics*, vol. 89, no. 9: 1743–1762.

Li, Jiayuan. 2015. "The Paradox of Performance Regimes: Strategic Responses to Target Regimes in Chinese Local Government." *Public Administration*, vol. 93, no. 4: 1152–1167.

Li, Ling. 2022. "China's 20th Party Congress: The Implications for CCP Norms: Revisiting the Resilience of the Age Limit Norm and Exploring Two Counterfactuals." *The Diplomat*, November 30. https://thediplomat .com/2022/11/chinas-20th-party-congress-the-implications-for-ccp-norms/.

Li, Xing, Chong Liu, Xi Weng, and Li-An Zhou. 2019. "Target Setting in Tournaments: Theory and Evidence from China." *Economic Journal*, vol. 129, no. 623: 2888–2915.

Li, Zeren, and Melanie Manion. 2023. "The Decline of Factions: The Impact of a Broad Purge on Political Decision-Making in China." *British Journal of Political Science*, vol. 53, no. 3: 815–834.

Liu, Hanzhang. 2018. "The Logic of Authoritarian Political Selection: Evidence from a Conjoint Experiment in China." *Political Science Research and Methods*, vol. 7, no. 4: 853–870.

Lorentzen, Peter L., and Xi Lu. 2018. "Personal Ties, Meritocracy, and China's Anti-Corruption Campaign." SSRN. http://dx.doi.org/10.2139/ssrn .2835841.

Lu, Fengming, and Xiao Ma. 2019. "Is Any Publicity Good Publicity? Media Coverage, Party Institutions, and Authoritarian Power-Sharing." *Political Communication*, vol. 36, no. 1: 64–82.

Lü, Xiaobo, and Pierre F. Landry. 2014. "Show Me the Money: Interjurisdiction Political Competition and Fiscal Extraction in China." *American Political Science Review*, vol. 108, no. 3: 706–722.

Ma, Damien, and Joshua Henderson. 2021. "Age Rules: The Arrival of the Post-60s Generation in Chinese Politics." *MacroPolo*, December 31. https://macro polo.org/analysis/post-60s-generation-chinese-politics/.

Ma, Liang. 2012. *Public Service Performance and Political Elite Career Advancement: Evidence from China*. Saarbrucken: Lambert Academic Publishing.

Ma, Liang, Huangfeng Tang, and Bo Yan. 2015. "Public Employees' Perceived Promotion Channels in Local China: Merit-Based or Guanxi-Orientated?" *Australian Journal of Public Administration*, vol. 74, no. 3: 283–297.

Manin, Bernard. 1997. *The Principles of Representative Government*. Cambridge: Cambridge University Press.

Manion, Melanie. 1985. "The Cadre Management System, Post-Mao: The Appointment, Promotion, Transfer and Removal of Party and State Leaders." *China Quarterly*, no. 102: 203–233.

Manion, Melanie. 1993. *Retirement of Revolutionaries in China: Public Policies, Social Norms, Private Interests*. Princeton, NJ: Princeton University Press.

Manion, Melanie. 2008. "When Communist Party Candidates Can Lose, Who Wins? Assessing the Role of Local People's Congresses in the Selection of Leaders in China." *China Quarterly*, no. 195: 607–630.

Manion, Melanie. 2015. "The Challenge of Corruption." In *China's Challenges*, edited by Jacques deLisle and Avery Goldstein, 125–138. Philadelphia: University of Pennsylvania Press.

Manion, Melanie. 2018. "The Role of the Organization Department in Political Selection." In *Zouping Revisited: Adaptive Governance in a Chinese County*, edited by Jean C. Oi and Steven M. Goldstein, 167–181. Stanford, CA: Stanford University Press.

Maskin, Eric, Yingyi Qian, and Chenggang Xu. 2000. "Incentives, Information, and Organizational Form." *Review of Economic Studies*, vol. 67, no. 2: 359–378.

Mayhew, David R. 1974. *Congress: The Electoral Connection*. New Haven, CT: Yale University Press.

Meyer, David, Victor C. Shih, and Jonghyuk Lee. 2016. "Factions of Different Stripes: Gauging the Recruitment Logics of Factions in the Reform Period." *Journal of East Asian Studies*, vol. 16, no. 1: 43–60.

Miller, Alice. 2012. "The Road to the 18th Party Congress." *China Leadership Monitor*, no. 36. www.hoover.org/sites/default/files/uploads/documents/CLM36AM.pdf.

Miyazaki, Ichisada. 1976. *China's Examination Hell: The Civil Service Examinations of Imperial China*, translated by Conrad Schirokauer. New Haven, CT: Yale University Press.

Montinola, Gabriella, Yingyi Qian, and Barry R. Weingast. 1995. "Federalism, Chinese Style: The Political Basis for Economic Success in China." *World Politics*, vol. 48, no. 1: 50–81.

Nathan, Andrew J. 1973. "A Factionalism Model for CCP Politics." *China Quarterly*, no. 53: 33–66.

Nathan, Andrew J., and Perry Link, eds. 2001. *The Tiananmen Papers: The Chinese Leadership's Decision to Use Force Against Their Own People – In Their Own Words*. Compiled by Zhang Liang. New York: Public Affairs.

Nathan, Andrew J., and Kellee S. Tsai. 1995. "Factionalism: A New Institutionalist Restatement." *China Journal*, no. 34: 157–192.

Naughton, Barry. 2007. *The Chinese Economy: Transitions and Growth*. Cambridge, MA: MIT Press.

Oi, Jean C. 1992. "Fiscal Reform and the Economic Foundations of Local State Corporatism in China." *World Politics*, vol. 45, no. 1: 99–126.

Ong, Lynette H. 2012. "Fiscal Federalism and Soft Budget Constraints: The Case of China." *International Political Science Review*, vol. 33, no. 4: 455–474.

Opper, Sonja, Victor Nee, and Stefan Brehm. 2015. "Homophily in the Career Mobility of China's Political Elite." *Social Science Research*, no. 54: 332–352.

Pang, Baoqing, Shu Keng, and Lingna Zhong. 2018. "Sprinting with Small Steps: China's Cadre Management and Authoritarian Resilience." *China Journal*, no. 80: 68–93.

Pieke, Frank N. 2009. *The Good Communist: Elite Training and State Building in Today's China*. Cambridge: Cambridge University Press.

Pines, Yuri. 2012. *The Everlasting Empire: The Political Culture of Ancient China and Its Imperial Legacy*. Princeton, NJ: Princeton University Press.

Pye, Lucian. 1980. *The Dynamic of Factions and Consensus in Chinese Politics: A Model and Some Propositions*. Santa Monica, CA: Rand.

Pye, Lucian. 1981. *The Dynamics of Chinese Politics*. Cambridge, MA: Oelgeschlager, Gunn, & Hain.

Qian, Yingyi, and Chenggang Xu. 1993. "Why China's Economic Reforms Differ: The M-Form Hierarchy and Entry/Expansion of the Non-State Sector." *Economics of Transition*, vol. 1, no. 2: 135–170.

Quinlivan, James T. 1999. "Coup-Proofing: Its Practice and Consequences in the Middle East." *International Security*, vol. 24, no. 2: 131–165.

Rui, Guo. 2022. "China's Communist Party Nears 97 Million, With More Younger and Educated Members." *South China Morning Post*, June 20. www.scmp.com/news/china/politics/article/3183669/chinas-communist-party-grows-near-97-million-its-made-younger.

Sheng, Yumin. 2010. *Economic Openness and Territorial Politics in China.* Cambridge: Cambridge University Press.

Sheng, Yumin. 2022. "Performance-Based Authoritarianism Revisited: GDP Growth and the Political Fortunes of China's Political Leaders." *Modern China*, vol. 48, no. 5: 982–1018.

Shi, Xiangyu, and Tianyang Xi. 2018. "Race to Safety: Political Competition, Neighborhood Effects, and Coal Mine Deaths in China." *Journal of Development Economics*, vol. 131: 79–95.

Shih, Victor, Christopher Adolph, and Mingxing Liu. 2012. "Getting Ahead in the Communist Party: Explaining the Advancement of Central Committee Members in China." *American Political Science Review*, vol. 106, no. 1: 166–187.

Shih, Victor, Wei Shan, and Mingxing Liu. 2010. "The Central Committee, Past and Present: A Method of Quantifying Elite Biographies." In *Contemporary Chinese Politics: New Sources, Methods, and Field Strategies*, edited by Mary E. Gallagher, Allen Carlson, Kenneth Lieberthal, and Melanie Manion, 51–68. Cambridge: Cambridge University Press.

Shirk, Susan L. 1993. *The Political Logic of Economic Reform in China.* Berkeley: University of California Press.

Shirk, Susan L. 2023. *Overreach: How China Derailed Its Peaceful Rise.* Oxford: Oxford University Press.

Smith, Graeme. 2009. "Political Machinations in a Rural County." *China Journal*, no. 62: 29–59.

Smith, Graeme. 2013. "Measurement, Promotions and Patterns of Behavior in Chinese Local Government." *Journal of Peasant Studies*, vol. 40, no. 6: 1027–1050.

Su, Fubing, Ran Tao, Lu Xi, and Ming Li. 2012. "Local Officials' Incentives and China's Economic Growth: Tournament Thesis Reexamined and Alternative Explanatory Framework." *China and World Economy*, vol. 20, no. 4: 1–18.

Sudduth, Jun Koga. 2017. "Strategic Logic of Elite Purges in Dictatorships." *Comparative Political Studies*, vol. 50, no. 13: 1768–1801.

Svolik, Milan W. 2012. *The Politics of Authoritarian Rule.* Cambridge: Cambridge University Press.

Tsou, Tang. 1995. "Chinese Politics at the Top: Factionalism or Informal Politics? Balance-of-Power Politics or a Game to Win All?" *China Journal*, no. 34: 95–156.

Tullock, Gordon. 1987. *Autocracy.* Dordrecht: Martinus Nijhoff Publishers.

Wallace, Jeremy. 2016. "Juking the Stats? Authoritarian Information Problems in China." *British Journal of Political Science*, vol. 46, no. 1: 11–29.

Wang, Yuhua, and Carl F. Minzner. 2015. "The Rise of the Security State." *China Quarterly*, no. 222: 339–359.

Whitford, Andrew B. 2002. "Bureaucratic Discretion, Agency Structure, and Democratic Responsiveness: The Case of the United States Attorneys." *Journal of Public Administration Research and Theory*, vol. 12, no. 1: 3–27.

Whiting, Susan. 1995. "The Micro-Foundations of Institutional Change in Reform China: Property Rights and Revenue Extraction in the Rural Industrial Sector." PhD dissertation, University of Michigan.

Whiting, Susan. 2000. *Power and Wealth in Rural China: The Political Economy of Institutional Change*. Cambridge: Cambridge University Press.

Whiting, Susan. 2004. "The Cadre Evaluation System at the Grass Roots: The Paradox of Party Rule." In *Holding China Together: Diversity and National Integration in the Post-Deng Era*, edited by Barry Naughton and Dali Yang, 101–119. Cambridge: Cambridge University Press.

Wiebe, Michael. 2020a. "Does Meritocratic Promotion Explain China's Growth?" Doctoral dissertation, chapter 1. University of British Columbia. https://michaelwiebe.com/assets/ch1.pdf.

Wiebe, Michael. 2020b. "Replicating the Literature on Meritocratic Promotion in China." Doctoral dissertation, chapter 2. University of British Columbia. https://michaelwiebe.com/assets/ch2.pdf.

Williamson, Oliver E. 1975. *Markets and Hierarchies, Analysis and Antitrust Implications: A Study in the Economics of Internal Organization*. New York: Free Press.

Wong, Stan Hok-Wui, and Yu Zeng. 2018. "Getting Ahead by Getting on the Right Track: Horizontal Mobility in China's Political Selection Process." *Journal of Contemporary China*, vol. 27, no. 109: 61–84.

Wu, Guoguang. 2015. *China's Party Congress: Power, Legitimacy, and Institutional Manipulation*. Cambridge: Cambridge University Press.

Xu, Chenggang. 2011. "The Fundamental Institutions of China's Reforms and Development." *Journal of Economic Literature*, vol. 49, no. 4: 1076–1151.

Yan, Huai. 1995. "Organizational Hierarchy and the Cadre Management System." In *Decision-Making in Deng's China: Perspectives from Insiders*, edited by Carol Lee Hamrin and Suisheng Zhao, 39–50. Armonk, NY: M. E. Sharpe.

Yan, Yang, and Chunhui Yuan. 2020. "City Administrative Level and Municipal Party Secretaries' Promotion: Understanding the Logic of Shaping Political Elites in China." *Journal of Contemporary China*, vol. 29, no. 122: 266–285.

Yao, Yang, and Muyang Zhang. 2015. "Subnational Leaders and Economic Growth: Evidence from Chinese Cities." *Journal of Economic Growth*, vol. 20, no. 4: 405–436.

Zeng, Qingjie. 2016. "Democratic Procedures in the CCP's Cadre Selection Process: Implementation and Consequences." *China Quarterly*, no. 225: 73–99.

Zeng, Yu, and Stan Hok-wui Wong. 2021. "Time Is Power: Rethinking Meritocratic Political Selection in China." *China Quarterly*, no. 245: 23–50.

Zhao, Ziyang. 2009. *Prisoner of the State: The Secret Journal of Premier Zhao Ziyang*, translated and edited by Bao Pu, Renee Chiang, and Adi Ignatius. New York: Simon and Schuster.

Zhong, Yang. 2003. *Local Government and Politics in China: Challenges from Below.* Studies on Contemporary China. Armonk, NY: M. E. Sharpe.

Zhou, Li-An. 2007. "Governing China's Local Officials: An Analysis of Promotion Tournament Model." *Economic Research Journal*, vol. 7: 36–50.

Zhu, Hongshen. 2022. "Constructive Conflict in China: Managing Policy Tradeoffs Under Authoritarianism." SSRN. http://dx.doi.org/10.2139/ssrn .4274576.

Zhu, Jiangnan. 2008. "Why Are Offices for Sale in China? A Case Study of the Office-Selling Chain in Heilongjiang Province." *Asian Survey*, vol. 48, no. 4: 558–579.

Zuo, Cai (Vera). 2015. "Promoting City Leaders: The Structure of Political Incentives in China." *China Quarterly*, no. 224: 955–984.

Acknowledgments

This Element is a product of my fascination, since graduate student days, with Chinese Communist Party control over the careers of anyone remotely important in China and my interest in the focus and findings of the more recent literature on political selection in China. Out of this grew a reading group with my graduate students at Duke University several years ago. Together, we discussed the substance and methods of several works I consider in Section 2. It is my great pleasure to express my heartfelt appreciation to participants in that reading group: Haohan Chen, Xiaoshu Gui, David Kearney, Zeren Li, Peng Peng, Jason Todd, Peiyu Wei, Jingyi Zhang, and Hongshen Zhu. In addition, for research assistance at several points along the way, I thank Ying Chi, Zeren Li, Viola Rothschild, and Hongshen Zhu. I am also very grateful to two anonymous reviewers for their careful reading and helpful comments and to Erin Aeran Chung, Mary Alice Haddad, and Benjamin Read for their encouragement and patience.

Cambridge Elements ⁼

Politics and Society in East Asia

Erin Aeran Chung

The Johns Hopkins University

Erin Aeran Chung is the Charles D. Miller Professor of East Asian Politics in the Department of Political Science at the Johns Hopkins University. She specializes in East Asian political economy, migration and citizenship, and comparative racial politics. She is the author of *Immigration and Citizenship in Japan* (Cambridge, 2010, 2014; Japanese translation, Akashi Shoten, 2012) and *Immigrant Incorporation in East Asian Democracies* (Cambridge, 2020). Her research has been supported by grants from the Academy of Korean Studies, the Japan Foundation, the Japan Foundation Center for Global Partnership, the Social Science Research Council, and the American Council of Learned Societies.

Mary Alice Haddad

Wesleyan University

Mary Alice Haddad is the John E. Andrus Professor of Government, East Asian Studies, and Environmental Studies at Wesleyan University. Her research focuses on democracy, civil society, and environmental politics in East Asia as well as city diplomacy around the globe. A Fulbright and Harvard Academy scholar, Haddad is author of *Effective Advocacy: Lessons from East Asia's Environmentalists* (MIT, 2021), *Building Democracy in Japan* (Cambridge, 2012), and *Politics and Volunteering in Japan* (Cambridge, 2007), and co-editor of *Greening East Asia* (University of Washington, 2021), and *NIMBY is Beautiful* (Berghahn Books, 2015). She has published in journals such as *Comparative Political Studies, Democratization, Journal of Asian Studies*, and *Nonprofit and Voluntary Sector Quarterly*, with writing for the public appearing in the *Asahi Shimbun*, the *Hartford Courant*, and the *South China Morning Post*.

Benjamin L. Read

University of California, Santa Cruz

Benjamin L. Read is a professor of Politics at the University of California, Santa Cruz. His research has focused on local politics in China and Taiwan, and he also writes about issues and techniques in comparison and field research. He is author of *Roots of the State: Neighborhood Organization and Social Networks in Beijing and Taipei* (Stanford, 2012), coauthor of *Field Research in Political Science: Practices and Principles* (Cambridge, 2015), and co-editor of *Local Organizations and Urban Governance in East and Southeast Asia: Straddling State and Society* (Routledge, 2009). His work has appeared in journals such as *Comparative Political Studies, Comparative Politics, the Journal of Conflict Resolution, the China Journal, the China Quarterly*, and *the Washington Quarterly*, as well as several edited books.

About the Series

The Cambridge Elements series on Politics and Society in East Asia offers original, multidisciplinary contributions on enduring and emerging issues in the dynamic region of East Asia by leading scholars in the field. Suitable for general readers and specialists alike, these short, peer-reviewed volumes examine common challenges and patterns within the region while identifying key differences between countries. The series consists of two types of contributions: 1) authoritative field surveys of established concepts and themes that offer roadmaps for further research; and 2) new research on emerging issues that challenge conventional understandings of East Asian politics and society. Whether focusing on an individual country or spanning the region, the contributions in this series connect regional trends with points of theoretical debate in the social sciences and will stimulate productive interchanges among students, researchers, and practitioners alike.

Cambridge Elements $^{\equiv}$

Politics and Society in East Asia

Elements in the Series

The East Asian Covid-19 Paradox
Yves Tiberghien

State, Society and Markets in North Korea
Andrew Yeo

The Digital Transformation and Japan's Political Economy
Ulrike Schaede, Kay Shimizu

Japan as a Global Military Power: New Capabilities, Alliance Integration, Bilateralism-Plus
Christopher W. Hughes

State and Social Protests in China
Yongshun Cai, Chih-Jou Jay Chen

The State and Capitalism in China
Margaret M. Pearson, Meg Rithmire, Kellee S. Tsai

A full series listing is available at: www.cambridge.org/EPEA

Printed in the United States
by Baker & Taylor Publisher Services